ESSAYS ON TEACHING SOCIAL STUDIES

Books by **Marlow Ediger** *and*
Digumarti Bhaskara Rao

Administration of Schools
Community Colleges
Curriculum Organisation
Curriculum of School Subjects
Effective Schooling
Effective School Curriculum
Elementary Curriculum
Elementary Curriculum Improvement
Essays on Teaching Mathematics
Essays on Teaching Science
Essays on Teaching Social Studies
Essays on Teaching Reading
Essays on Teaching and Learning
Improving School Administration
Issues in School Curriculum
Language Arts Curriculum
Philosophy and Curriculum
Psychology and Curriculum
Quality School Education
Reading Curriculum and Instruction
Relevancy in Elementary Curriculum
School Organisation
School Curriculum and Administration
Science Curriculum
Teaching English Successfully
Teaching Language Arts Successfully
Teaching Mathematics Successfully
Teaching Science Successfully
Teaching Social Studies Successfully
Teaching Mathematics in Elementary Schools
Teaching Science in Elementary Schools
Successful School Administration
Successful School Education

published by
Discovery Publishing House

ESSAYS ON TEACHING SOCIAL STUDIES

by

DR. MARLOW EDIGER
Emeritus Professor of Education
Truman State University
P.O. Box 417, 201 W 22nd St
North Newton KS 67117
United States of America

&

Dr. Digumarti Bhaskara Rao
Reader and Research Director
R.V.R. College of Education
D-43 (277) S.V.N. Colony
Guntur - 522006, India

DISCOVERY PUBLISHING HOUSE PVT. LTD.

NEW DELHI-110 002

Published by:
Tilak Wasan
DISCOVERY PUBLISHING HOUSE PVT. LTD.
4831/24, Prahlad Street, Ansari Road
Darya Ganj, New Delhi-110002 (India)
Phone: +91-11-23279245, 43764432
Fax: +91-11-23253475
E-mail: parul.wasan@gmail.com
discoverypublishinghouse@gmail.com
info@discoverypublishinggroup.com
web: www.discoverypublishinggroup.com

***First Edition:* 2011**
ISBN: 978-81-8356-883-8

Essays on Teaching Social Studies

Printed at:
Shree Balaji Art Press
Delhi

Dedicated
to

Harshitha Digumarthi

Preface

Social studies is the integrated study of the social sciences and humanities to promote civic competence. It is most commonly recognized as the name of a course or set of courses taught in schools, but may also refers to the study of particular aspects of human society around the globe. At the elementary school level, social studies generally focuses first on the local community and family. By middle and high school, the social studies curriculum becomes more discipline-based and content-specific. It includes various fields which involve past and current human behavior and interactions, such as sociology, history, political science, economics, religion, geography, anthropology, and civics. Now the teaching of social studies is made a school subject across the world and such subject needs successful teaching.

In the successful teaching of social studies, the teaching learning equipment, the teacher, the curriculum, the library, the social studies laboratory, the academic atmosphere, the teaching-learning programmes, etc., play their legitimate role.

This book will be of great use to curriculum designers and teachers and administrators.

Digumarti Bhaskara Rao
digumartibhaskararao@redeiffmail.com

Sri Sai Soudha
D-43 S.V.N. Colony
Guntur 522006
India

Contents

Teacher and Students in Social Studies

1

There are selected ideas from the psychology of learning which assists students to achieve more optimally. They need to be in the repertoire of the social studies teacher. These are self-efficacy, resilience, reflection, and self-monitoring of the learner's own progress. Each of these concepts will be discussed as it relates to teaching and learning situations in the social studies.

Salient Concepts in Teaching Social Studies

Feelings of self-efficacy is highly important for teachers to develop in order to teach effectively. This emphasizes that the teacher feels confident that he/she can assist students to do well in the social studies. Subject-matter knowledge as well as skills are possessed to do a good job of teaching. Feelings of confidence make it increasingly possible to offer a quality social studies curriculum. Teachers feel that they can make an immense difference in students achieving stated objectives. The feelings, too, are that the learning opportunities provided assist students to be engaged in purposeful learning. Evaluation will indicate the degree to which students have achieved the objectives of instruction. Being confident in oneself is salient in teaching students. Learners develop selected perceptions of the teacher. Having confidence in the teacher's ability to teach well should assist more optimal achievement (Ediger, 2007).

The social studies teacher then needs to do much studying and reflecting upon social science content as well as in methods of teaching. A good personal or school library housing professional journals and teacher education textbooks facilitate, in their reading, to becoming a true professional in teaching the social studies. Additional approaches in becoming increasingly competent in teaching the social studies include :

- working toward an advanced degree at an accredited university
- taking courses online from a reputable university
- doing a research study on an important problem area in teaching the social studies
- completing an independent study on trends and issues in the social sciences/social studies
- attending professional conferences such as the annual and regional conferences of the National Council for the Social Studies
- video taping segments of one's own teaching and then analyzing it into component parts to notice what might be improved upon. Colleagues may help in the assessment of the video (Santiago *et al.,* 2008).

As the teacher grows, develops, and achieves in subject-matter knowledge and in methods of teaching, he/she tends to become more efficacious. Self-efficacy indicates confidence in being highly competent to teach well regardless of ability and income levels of students involved.

Resilience and the Student

A very good characteristic for all to develop is resilience. To the writer, resilience emphasizes bouncing back after experiencing defeat. The bouncing back stresses continual attempts at reaching upward toward a relevant goal. An unpleasant experience does not keep the resilient person from trying again and again, with success in the offing. There are individuals who feel defeated if they do not succeed in achieving a selected goal. There may even be feelings of bitterness in making attempts at achievement. A resilient person tends to learn from unpleasant efforts and modifies behaviour to account for future success. Failure tends to be a learning experience. Deficiencies are evaluated and new procedures used to make for success in the ensuing endeavor. Many a times the feeling is if one fails, no other chances are given to succeed. The resilient person makes choices in life. The choices involved are numerous. It may be choices among good possibilities. It might also be choices between the lesser of two evils, unfortunately. Some are born in very unfortunate circumstances such as poverty, and yet they become highly successful in life. The opposite is true also that individuals born in very fortunate circumstances, do poorly in life. Life is not too friendly to some. However, one thing is true, whatever the present circumstance of the individual, the kinds of decisions made have much relevance for the future. In looking at pictures of graduates in a daily newspaper, the writer wonders what will happen to these young people as they pursue life in different areas of higher/technical education and at the work place. Defeat will be experienced along the way, but can these individuals rise above negative situations in life? Resilience is important and might well be fostered in school through

- being treated fairly and politely by students and teachers
- experiencing success in different academic as well as non-academic course work
- eliminating harassment and abuse in school. Name calling, rudeness, intimidation, and reminding individuals of their failures should be a thing of the past!

- meaningful course work and providing assistance to any student needing help to be successful on his/her developmental level.
- helping students individually to achieve as optimally as possible (Booker, 2008).

Monitoring Achievement and Reflection

One highly salient skill for student achievement, among others, is to monitor one's own progress in reading social studies subject-matter. There are students who read content, but cannot say what was read in terms of ideas. If the subject-matter is developmental appropriate, the reader should be able to understand what was read. Developmentally appropriate means that the content read is on the understanding level of the reader. Approximately, 95 per cent of the running words are then identified correctly as well as three of four questions covering subject matter read are answered correctly.

As the student reads social studies content, he/she reflects upon what was read. Understanding of subject-matter read is being emphasized in the skill of reflection. Thus, the learner is monitoring if comprehension is taking place. With the act of monitoring, the learner checks his/her progress. Monitoring may also take place when reflecting upon ideas having been discussed. The student is then taking stock if he/she attached meaning to what was being discussed. Reflection may also involve higher levels of cognition, such as pondering upon ideas read/discussed. Critical thinking may then be emphasized when separating facts from opinions, fantasy from reality, and accurate from inaccurate statements. Reflection may also be stressed when the leaner thinks of creative solutions to problem areas such as in the following, based upon student readiness factors :

- devastating effects of tornados and hurricanes in different areas of the world with remediation endeavors to remedy the destructive happenings.

- problems of health care and their solutions.
- drug misuse and how to rehabilitate affected persons.
- the prison population and attempts at rehabilitation
- improving educational opportunities and schooling for students and the lay population in general.
- minimizing harmful effects of green house gases.
- ways of leading an enriched life for all with a plethora of opportunities for self fulfilment.
- meeting esteem needs of individuals and groups.
- emphasizing the need to belong to as well as being accepted in groups in the societal arena.

For each of the above, the social studies teacher needs to have a quality current events program in developing student hypotheses/solutions to the Iraqi war and the Middle East in general. Current events in the social studies should also stress the identification of problem areas on the state, national, and international scenes. A problem solving approach is recommended whereby students with teacher guidance consider problems in health care, drug abuse, inmate rehabilitation programmes, as well as considering programs for meeting educational needs, and problems in green house gases. The psychological needs of esteem and recognition should be considered carefully as well as the need to belong in society. Each of these areas may serve as objectives to achieve. Learning activities to achieve the objectives involving problem solving include the following :

- use of the internet within cooperative experiences for students.
- use of daily newspapers, news magazines, TV and radio news broadcasts.
- resource personnel who specialize in a relevant area of expertise.
- excursions, debates, discussions, seminars, as well as peer teaching and learning.

- textbooks, library books, and encyclopaedias.
- audio presentations directly related to the problem being considered (Ediger, 2008).

To appraise achievement, the following need to be used to assess progress. Teacher observation should be used continuously to note achievement of objectives. Observational facets include on task behavior of learners. Student active engagement in ongoing learning opportunities needs adequate emphasis. Sequential progress of each student is a must! Teacher written test items provide further feedback in noticing student achievement. These include essay and multiple choice test items. Oral communication such as discussions also provide feedback of what students have learned in the social studies. The feedback should provide information on what each student has left to learn.

Portfolios developed by students with teacher guidance are useful to communicate learnings to parents. They contain representative work of a student in the social studies such as written and recorded book reports, art work as it relates to an ongoing unit of study, snapshots and digital photos of construction projects completed, among others (Owens and Peltier, 2002).

REFERENCES

Booker, Keonya, (2008), 'The Role of Instructors and Peers in Establishing Classroom Community," *Journal of Instructional Psychology*, 35 (1), 12-16.

Ediger, Marlow (2007), "Developing an Appreciation for the Social Studies," *Edutracks,* 7(1), 5-7.

Ediger, Marlow (2008), "Current Events, the Student, and the Social Studies," *Florida Council for the Social Studies Newsletter,* 1-5.

Owens, Terry, and Gary Peltier, (2002), "Communicating with Parents, Parental Perceptions, of State School Accountability Reporting," *Education* 122 (3), 595-599.

Santiago, Eileen, *et al.*, "A Full Service School Fulfills Its Responsibilities," *Educational Leadership*, 65 (7), 44-49.

Collaboration in Teaching Social Studies

2

Much is written about the need for collaboration in developing the social studies curriculum. Teachers need to work together harmoniously in selecting the best objectives, learning opportunities, and appraisal procedures. Too frequently, the same design is used over and over again without critically evaluating the social studies programme. With collaborative endeavors, each social studies teacher may benefit from interacting with others in curricular endeavours. What might be accomplished in working together?

Collaboration in the Social Studies

Together, teachers may plan and work collectively on devising a quality social studies curriculum. The objectives section might well be a starting point. Critical and creative thinking by teachers is necessary to solve relevant problems. The objectives section needs to be evaluated in terms of the following :

- do they emphasize subject-matter which is salient and significant? Trivia and the unimportant may thus be weeded out.

- are vital facts, concepts, and generalizations organized sequentially?
- is subject-matter integrated with other academic disciplines when it is relevant to do so?
- does the scope clearly indicate the breadth of content to be studied by leaners?
- are the objectives stated as precisely as possible so that pupil achievement may be evaluated in terms of these chosen ends of instruction?
- is there a balance between subject matter and skills objectives?
- are attitudinal objectives stressed adequately?

It is complex to determine answers to each of the above; however, adequate attention must be given to develop a quality social studies curriculum. With collaboration, participant social studies teachers analyze the present units of study being taught. There is then a renewed interest in subject-matter, skills, and attitudes which comprise teaching and learning situations. Discussing each of these areas provide for growth and achievement among social studies teachers. Reflective thinking of one's own personal experiences in teaching also identifies problems and issues in curriculum development. New, agreed upon objectives need to be tried out in the classroom with results being reported back to the collaborative team members. After analysis, synthesis must be emphasized by combining results from analytic situations.

The learning opportunities, for collaborative study, may be combined with the objectives in teaching social studies. Learning opportunities are chosen to be aligned with the objectives. They need to be varied to provide for diverse levels of pupil achievement as well as different styles of learning. Pupils differ from each other in a plethora of ways and the needs of learners must be met with high quality, rich learning opportunities. The following need to be examined indepth, collaboratively by teachers of social studies, and solutions found pertaining to implementing quality learning opportunities for pupils :

- inductive versus deductive learning.
- large group, small groups, and individual study for pupils as compared to teaching the class as a whole.
- learning by discovery versus use of lecture/ explanations in ongoing lessons and units of study.
- problem-solving and project methods as compared to more traditional approaches of teaching.
- use of technology to upgrade the social studies curriculum as compared to a more heavy emphasis upon textbooks, workbooks, and work sheets.

Learning opportunities need to provide for individual differences. They also must be meaningful and make sense to the learner. Pupils need to be fully engaged and be assisted in developing interest in each lesson. It is also salient for learners to perceive purpose or reasons for learning. Objectives must reflect what is relevant in school and in society. Collaborative endeavours should assist teachers to become efficacious and confident in their ability to teach well. An adequate self concept is necessary for this to occur.

Appraisal techniques must be valid and reliable. They must measure if pupils have achieved vital objectives. The following evaluation procedures need to be used to ascertain if social studies objectives have been attained:

- teacher written tests to measure achievement in ongoing lessons and units of study.
- these tests need to be formative to ascertain pupil progress within a unit of study as well as summative or end of unit tests. Benchmark tests might well determine if pupils have achieved selected goals at a particular time within a unit of study.

- mandated tests given annually to evaluate learner progress.
- teacher observation to detect misunderstandings and needed corrections made as a social studies lesson progresses.
- self-evaluation by pupils in terms of desired criteria.

Collaborative endeavours can do much to improve all facets of teaching social studies, including the evaluation procedures. Self-evaluation by teachers is important and answers to the following questions need to be pursued :

- do I reflect upon my teaching to notice what works and what needs to be improved upon?
- am I growing as a professional in teaching the social studies?
- will pupils be adequately prepared to live as citizens in a democracy?
- is there balance among the different social science disciplines which comprise the social studies?
- do learners experience a relevant curriculum?
- did social studies teachers work together harmoniously in collaborative endeavors?
- are pupil interests in social studies growing?
- do they ask stimulating questions?
- do learners perceive authentic purposes for teaching and learning situations?
- am I developing feelings of self efficacy?

When teachers work in collaborative situations, they need to have access to quality library materials. A special section of the school library needs to house social studies teaching journals, university textbooks in teaching the social studies, video-tapes showing classrooms in action, and recordings of teaching the social studies by professors from diverse universities.

Collaborative Approach in Teaching the Social Studies

Social studies teachers who have appraised the total curriculum may also volunteer to teach collaboratively. Collective decision making without a designated leader emphasizes the following :

- leadership emerges as ideas are expressed for daily lesson plans and units of instruction. Each participant becomes a leader as he/she presents ideas for objectives, learning opportunities, and appraisal procedures. In evaluating the worth of each, the total group is involved in planning.
- content for the discussion comes from personal experiences, research data, journal articles, and university teaching social studies textbooks, among others. Examining ideas involves critical thinking, creative thinking in coming up with new ideas, as well as problem-solving.
- assessment of ideas are based in their individual worth for developing a worthwhile program of social studies. The subject-matter must be useful to pupils presently as well as in society, in developing citizens who work toward improving society.
- teachers, individually or collectively, may volunteer to teach the class as a whole. Strengths of teachers must be used here on a rotation basis. Small group instruction needs to follow and involves all social studies teachers who collaborated in curriculum development. Pupils also need to select and work on individual projects, supervised by these same teachers.
- evaluation of pupil progress must involve all members of the collaborative teaching approach. A variety of valid and reliable methods should be used. These include teacher observation, mandated testing results, standardized tests, and teacher written tests such as multiple choice, essay, and short answer. Results from

pupil evaluation should feed instruction. Thus, social studies teachers must use evaluative findings to improve instruction such as in the following :

(*a*) specific subject-matter misunderstandings

(*b*) skills missing in pupil's repertoire-reading information from different kinds of maps and globes, locating information from reference sources including the internet and world wide web, writing summaries and conclusions, active participation in discussions and oral communication activities, and reading for a variety of purposes.

(*c*) areas of critical and creative thinking, and problem solving as well as metacognition which need more emphasis.

- resource personnel, such as university social science/ social studies professors should also have ample input, when possible, in developing a viable curriculum. A series of meetings planned with these professors may well provide impetus, also, in working toward curriculum improvement.

CONCLUSIONS

Collaboration involves working together to develop a quality social studies curriculum. Designing lessons and units of study assists in determining scope and sequence in the social studies. Collaborative teaching further stresses the importance of using talents and skills of teachers. The following are benefits of working well with others in collaborative endeavors in the social studies :

- participants learn from each other to improve teaching quality
- more than one mind is better than a single mind to determine relevance

- teacher support is necessary to implement and appraise the social studies curriculum. Many knowledgeable persons should be involved in curriculum improvement, including school administrators, curriculum directors, and lay people/parents.

Social studies instruction is important for all since it involves developing a good citizen with all the necessary inherent qualities needed and being developed subsequently in ongoing lessons and units of study.

3 Teaching Social Studies in Modern World of Agriculture

Few people make a living from farming. Estimates are that approximately less than two per cent do so. Children in small town public schools may no longer even have grandparents or great grandparents who were farmers. At the time of the American Revolutionary War, about 95 per cent were living on and making a living from farming. What has happened to make for the decrease? Technology has made for tremendous improvements and made individual farmers highly productive, making less of a need for people to derive a livelihood from agriculture.

When the writer was in high school, 1942-1946, his father farmed 160 acres of farm land, had 300 laying hens to produce eggs for selling, milked 17 dairy cows by hand, and raised 20 hogs per year for market. Agriculture has made tremendous changes since that time. No farm producer milks that low number of dairy cows, raises so few pigs, or farms such small acreage today unless they also work at a paying job in a nearby area. This paper will focus on dairy farming as it is presently and how teachers in the social studies may use the information for an entire unit of study or to integrate into existing structures.

Teaching and Learning in the Social Studies

As a professor of education, the writer taught undergraduate courses in Teaching the Social Studies. Various procedures were used. One student in class developed a series of learning centres, each clearly labelled and with a task card of five learning activities. Students played the role of intermediate grade pupils in selecting which to pursue sequentially. At one centre, there were illustrations of a grandfather with two dairy cows, a milk pail, a cream can capable of holding ten gallons of milk or cream, a cream separator which separates cream from milk, and a wooden stall for feeding grain which was carried by hand in a half gallon container. When appraising that particular learning centre, most university students in the class of 25 believed that this presented an accurate picture of modern dairy farming. However, there were two university students who had considerable knowledge of a dairy farm today. The following emerged during the spirited discussion together with a followup, using a variety of research data and human resource personnel, which might well serve as objectives for learners to achieve in an entire social studies unit or integrated with another :

- the dairy industry is highly regulated for cleanliness and efficiency in using modern methods in the production of milk.
- cows are milked in a modern milking parlour (small dairy barn), which is kept very clean, whereby the udder of each is thoroughly washed and disinfected prior to being milked.
- electrically-operated milking machines are attached to each udder. Generally, there is a concrete lined pit from which the milking machine operator stands; this minimizes the continual bending over to attach the milking machine to each cow.
- the milk moves from the machine used to milk each dairy cow, via a plastic pipeline, to a bulk milk tank,

holding about a thousand gallons of milk. The milk is untouched by human hands.

- a dairy supplement (feed for each cow) is purchased and brought by a commercial company to one or more steel bins, located next to the dairy barn. It is then augured automatically to where each cow in the dairy barn is allotted her share of feed based on the amount of milk produced.
- careful electronic records are kept on each cow's amount of milk produced, since efficiency in productivity is necessary. Cow which lack in productivity are culled and sold.
- outside the dairy barn, cows are fed hay in the form of alfalfa and prairie grass. In the warm months, dairy cows also graze grass in the nearby available pasture land. The latter depends upon how much pasture land acreage is available.
- dairy farms vary much in size, from 100 to 1200 milk cows. An average cow will give, approximately, 15,000 pounds of milk per nine to ten month year. Cows not producing a calf during an approximate twelve month year are generally culled and sold.
- a commercial company picks up the milk from the dairy farm, regularly, and hauls it to a processing plant for placing the milk in a gallon or half gallon containers. An attached hose to the bulk milk tank vacuums the milk to the tank on the commercial truck. There are a plethora of by products made from milk such as ice cream, whipping cream, and butter, among others. These are transported to super markets for consumer purchase and consumption.

There are numerous learning activities which teachers may implement to assist pupils to achieve the above flexible objectives. The following are recommended, among others :

- illustrations and articles from the internet and world wide web, as well as from farm journals such as

Successful Farming, and Hoard's Dairyman provide subject-matter for reading and discussions.

- audio-visual aids from the local county agricultural farm agent's office may be viewed to identify problem areas.
- content, such as pictures, explanations, and models, supplied by a local dairyman with a large herd of milk cows, provides ideas from a primary source.
- textbook subject-matter on the developmental level of the learner may be analyzed, synthesized, and evaluated
- writing to dairy associations, addresses on the internet, for literature on Holstein, Jersey, Guernsey, Brown Swiss, and Milking Shorthorn, dairy cows. Doing a scrap book on different breeds of dairy animals is fascinating to many pupils.
- making models, drawings, and doing dioramas, based on research, involving milk production emphasizes a hands on approach in learning.
- dramatizing scenes from dairy farming, based on recent trends, breathes life into ongoing learning experiences.
- peer discussions involving separate facets on dairy farming might well stress social development of learners.
- identifying problem areas based on gaps in knowledge and securing needed information pertaining to each problem.
- doing committee and individual reports, written and oral, on dairy farming assists in developing the reading, writing, listening, and speaking vocabularies.

Evaluation of Achievement

A quality programme of evaluation assists the teacher to ascertain what has been learned and what is left to learn.

Self- evaluation by the teacher is salient such as the following:

1. did I help each child achieve as much as possible in knowledge, skills, and attitudes pertaining to dairy farming?
2. were pupils enthused in learning about dairy farming?
3. do learners understand what is involved in milk production?
4. are pupils intrinsically motivated to learn more about production, distribution, and consumption of milk?
5. what happens to profits of dairy farmers when overproduction of milk occurs?
6. which major problems are faced by farms engaged in producing milk?
7. do pupils understand the need for clean, sanitary procedures in producing milk?
8. did learners, as the unit progressed, understand which kinds of diseases cause decreased profits in dairy farming such as Bang's disease (premature birth of calves, mastitus in milk—pus infection in udders, and tuberculosis, among others)?
9. were pupils able to raise salient questions in doing research on producing milk?
10. is there an increase in using appropriate study skills, as well as effective attitudes in the ongoing unit of study?

Along with self-evaluation, valid and reliable teacher written tests such as multiple choice and essay tests might well assist to understand what pupils have/have not learned. Multiple choice should have four plausible distractors for each test item. They need to be of similar length so as not to provide clues as to which is correct. Essay tests need to be adequately delimited in terms of questions asked, but not so that facts are required only. They should stress problem solving, critical and creative thinking.

IN CONCLUSION

Most pupils do not know the origin of foods eaten. Thus a unit on dairy farming or incorporated into an ongoing unit of study might well provide learners with the information needed to understand where milk comes from and how it reaches the dinner table. Milk is a staple and has its many nutritional values. The dairy cow grazing in the pasture or in the milk parlor is a beginning in pupils understanding where milk in the supermarket comes from.

Children's Literature in Social Studies Curriculum 4

There are myriad library books written for children which may be incorporated into ongoing lessons and units in the social studies. These are written on different topics that individually may relate directly to objectives of instruction in the classroom setting. Library books need to be on diverse reading levels in order for a pupils to select one which is developmental appropriate. The social studies teacher must briefly tell about salient books that might well pique learner attention. Then too, the teacher may read aloud to children, during story time, a carefully chosen book which captures pupils[1] interests. Thus, there is much social studies subject matter that pupils may acquire from library book content (Ellery, 2010).

Library Book Content in the Social Studies

A neat, well-developed colorful bulletin board draws pupil attention to salient library books. While supervising university student teachers in the public schools, the writer observed four committee members plan and complete a library book bulletin board display Crepe paper of red and green provided the outline. The caption was titled, "Enjoying the Social Studies and Library Books". Jackets of new books were posted on the bulletin board. Underneath each was a brief description of the library book. The teacher introduced each book briefly as she pointed to the related book jacket. Proper voice inflection can do much to capture pupil interest. Thus, appropriate stress, pitch, and enunciation, entices learner attention. Not only new books may be introduced, but also fascinating older library copies should receive attention in the classroom. There are favorites among pupils which are read by a plethora of young learners. Bulletin boards should be changed frequently to encourage pupil reading. They may be developed by the teacher at the beginning of a school year. When readiness occurs, pupil/teacher planning might be used as well as a committee of learners being engaged in planning and doing these bulletin boards. Being on the lookout for bulletin board ideas is poignant to social studies teachers (Wyss, 2007).

There are numerous plans for having children read library books as well as methods of achievement evaluation :

- pupils choose and read library books from selections made by the teacher or school librarian, devoted to the social studies. The teacher observes which books and by whom these are read. Teacher observation and related records kept might be a good way to assess progress. There are pupils who thrive in an informal program of reading library books in the social studies.
- pupils select and read a library book and then have a brief conference with the social studies teacher. A random sampling of conferences provide much feedback on reading comprehension from questions asked by the teachers well as word recognition skills shown by a pupil in oral reading. The teacher dates and records specific information. Streamlining the approach makes for efficiency in the conference setting.
- pupils share ideas gleaned from reading library books during time devoted to the social studies, especially

if they relate to an ongoing lesson/unit of study (Ediger, 2010).

There are selected procedures available in assisting pupils who have difficulties in word recognition. Procedures must be adapted to the developmental level of the learner and include the following :

- **use of context clues :** Thus, an unknown word needs to harmonize in meaning with the rest of the words in the sentence or paragraph. Sometimes, a pupil will place a word in context which is ridiculous and does not make sense. Pupils may be aided in inserting a word which is meaningful for the unknown.
- **use of phonics :** Initial consonants, in particular, identified properly, provide strong clues in word recognition especially if used with context clues. They are generally very consistent in relating symbol and sound.
- use of picture clues which are heaviest in literature for young children. If a pupil is not able to recognize a word, the picture on the same page of print will fill in for the unknown.
- use of teacher or proficient pupil reader in pronouncing words for those who have difficulties in word recognition. Pupils should not lose interest in reading due to not identifying unknown words. Assisting pupils, almost immediately, in identifying the unknown, helps in reading comprehension (Ediger, 2007).

Comprehension of Subject-matter

There are pupils who read words but do not understand the inherent ideas. They are word callers and do not comprehend what has been read. It is good for the social studies teacher to periodically ask a pupil to say in his/her own words what was understood from his/her reading. Recalling, literally, subject-matter read is a beginning point in comprehension. This needs to be stressed prior to emphasizing higher levels of comprehension. Recall of subject-matter, ideally, must be operationalized when actual reading of words is being in evidence. Reading is worthless unless ideas are being gleaned. Cause and effect is next in complexity in comprehension and is enclosed in historical content. Thus for example in a unit on the Middle East, there are causes for effects such as the Palestinian/Israeli disagreements over the land of Palestine. Critical thinking, in sequence, must also be stressed. For example, how have previous plans failed in coming up with a solution to highly relevant situations? This is making comparisons in procedures and approaches. Creative thinking, also salient, would differ in that the pupil needs to come up with a unique solution between opposing sides in the conflict. There are additional types of thinking including :

- reading between the lines where the subject matter is not clear.
- reading to make comparisons and contrasts.
- reading to make predictions.

Reading subject-matter from basal social studies textbooks involves several readiness factors. The new vocabulary terms need to be introduced and observed on the white board. The act of reading becomes more meaningful when pupils view these concepts and discuss their meaning. All pupils should see the words clearly in order to recognize them while reading silently or aloud from the basal textbook. During the discussion, pupils raise questions which might be answered from reading the textbook selection. The salient questions, along with those of the teacher and printed on the white board, provide a structure for reading comprehension of subject matter.

IN SUMMARY

Children's literature in the social studies should be an integral part of unit planning and implementation in the curriculum.

Relevant information needs to be sought which captures and holds learner attention. Learning opportunities need to make sense and be meaningful. Pupil purposes, also, need adequate consideration in curriculum development (Parker, 2001).

REFERENCES

Ediger, Marlow (1999), *The Holy Land.* Kirksville, Missouri: Simpson Publishing Company.

Ediger, Marlow (2007), "Meaning in Reading Instruction," *Reading Improvement,* 44 (4), 217-220.

Ediger, Marlow (2010), "Constructivism and the Social Studies," *Edutracks*, 9(7), 13-14.

Ellery, Valerie (2010), "How Do We Teach Reading as a Strategic Decision Making Process?" *The Reading Teacher*, 63 (5), 434-436.

National Council for the Social Studies (1997), *Curriculum Standards for the Social Studies.* Edison, New York : Whitehurst and Clark.

Parker, Walter C., (2001), *Social Studies in Elementary Education.* Upper Saddle River, New Jersey : Merrill, Prentice-Hall.

Wyss, Paul Alan (2007),"Solving the Problem of Distance Library Services," *College Student Journal*, 41 (4), 747-754.

Scope and Sequence in Social Studies - Revisited

5

With federal mandates in education (No Child Left Behind), social studies instruction was greatly minimized since it was not tested in pupil achievement. Restoring social studies to its rightful place is salient due to its relevance for pupils. Quality citizenship should be a major objective of instruction and this concept may be integrated in all its of study. Being a good citizen in school and in society is necessary for optimal achievement to occur. Disruptive behavior, rudeness, and impoliteness have no roles to play in a quality curriculum.

The social studies teacher has an important responsibility to determine with other teachers the breadth and depth (scope) as well as order (sequence) of units to be taught on a given grade level. Planning each lesson and unit of study is salient so that pupils achieve more optimally in the school setting (Ediger, 2007).

Planning the Framework in the Social Studies

Scope will be discussed first. What will be decided upon as the breadth of subject matter to be emphasized in ongoing lessons and units of study? If, for example, a unit on the Middle East is being considered, which concepts and generalizations will be stressed as objectives of instruction? The social studies teacher may choose to include the nations of Jordan, Israel, and the West Bank, as part of a unit of study on the Middle East. The following might be key structural ideas identified in terms of knowledge objectives :

- the West Bank of the Jordan River was a part of the nation of Jordan from 1948 until 1967.
- the West Bank contains 20 per cent of the land formerly called Palestine. Thus 80 per cent became the nation of Israel in 1948. A cease-fire in this Arab/Israeli war set the boundaries in 1948.
- in 1967, Israel captured the rest of the West Bank from Jordan in what is known as the six-day war.
- the walled city of Jerusalem was located on the West Bank. This wall, the third in its history, was completed in 1542 when the Ottoman Empire governed the land of Palestine from 1517-1917. The Ottoman Empire was defeated in World War I. Great Britain received the League of Nations Mandate to rule the land of Palestine in 1922, after the negotiations were completed following World War I.
- The walled city contains salient sites important to Islam, Judaism, and Christianity. The Dome of the Rock, an octagonal building with a gold plaited dome, was built in AD 691, after the Muslims captured the land of Palestine. It houses Mount Moriah, the site where the Patriarch Abraham was tempted to offer as a sacrifice his son Isaac, according to Judaism, whereby, in Islam, Abraham was tempted to sacrifice his son Ishmael. Isaac is considered the father of Judaism, and Ishmael, the father of the Arab nations. From the Dome, a Muezzin calls devout Muslims to prayer five times a day; also nearby, the Prophet Mohammed made his midnight journey into heaven and came back to earth again, according to devout followers of Islam.

- the Western Wall, located adjacent to the Dome of the Rock, is the only remains of the ancient Jewish temple, built during the days of Herod the Great. Here, devout Jews come to pray daily. Herod the Great ruled Palestine from 30 BC to 3 BC when the Roman Empire was at its zenith in power.
- inside the waited city is the Church of the Holy Sepulchre which houses the Tomb of Christ. The Church was built by the Crusaders in 1142 after they had captured most of the Holy Land from the Muslims in 1099. It houses also the place of one of three crosses from which Christ was crucified, according to devout beliefs of Christians (Ediger, 1998).

The walled city of Jerusalem was a part of the nation of Jordan until Israel captured it along with the West Bank in the 1967 six-day war. The above asterisked items may be stated as objectives for pupil attainment. The scope might well be broadened to include the Sea of Galilee, as well as the Dead Sea, among many, many others. For example, in the northwest where the Dead Sea and the Jordan river intersect are the remains of the Esscenes, a communal, religious group who separated themselves from others. The remains show a communal kitchen where Esscene members shared meals, a scriptorium room for writing religious texts, a storage area for food, and sleeping quarters. Stone slabs were slept upon with stone pillows to elevate the head. Even with scant rainfall of less than five inches a year, the Esscenes each day followed a purification ritual by dipping into an adjacent pool. Esscene society came to an end, approximately AD 100, when the Roman Army captured this settlement.

The scope of the social studies must be carefully determined. The breadth of subject-matter to be emphasized in teaching and learning situations adequately delimits a unit of study to be stressed in ongoing lessons and units of study. This makes for a planned balance in content from the social sciences with other social studies units (Parker, 2001).

Sequence in the Social Studies

Equally poignant is the concept of sequence. Here, the teacher determines the order of units to be taught as well as sequential learning activities to be emphasized within a unit of study. The authors, here, will discuss the order of learning activities to be provided within a unit. Thus, the teacher must provide for individual differences among learners so that each might attain optimally. Scaffolding is salient in that a pupil or group might well attain a higher level than what is developmentally appropriate. For example, the pupil may be able to achieve objective A, but objective B is too complicated unless scaffolding is used as a teaching strategy. With scaffolding, the teacher assists pupils to attain more optimally with a series of learning opportunities which challenge the pupil to realize higher levels of achievement in smaller steps. The social studies teacher must carefully evaluate pupil achievement within a lesson to help when this becomes necessary. Teacher observation is very important when teaching pupils to notice where assistance is necessary. Inductively, the teacher may raise questions which lead a pupil to a more accurate understanding of subject matter or a skill when the learner needs guidance (National Council for the Social Studies, 1997).

The social studies teacher has selected guidelines to follow in teaching to optimize sequential pupil progress :

- pupils need to be actively involved in learning. Distractions hinder achievement and progress. The classroom climate must be such that it encourages learning. Rules need to be established and communicated clearly to learners. Violations need to be treated in a humane way. The social studies teacher must think of methods of discipline which encourage learning and achievement. Active involvement in learning means that the interests of pupils must be considered. There are methods to make any topic or lesson interesting. Vary the kinds of experiences provided and include stimulating discussions, use of age appropriate audio-visual materials, art work to indicate what has been acquired in knowledge objectives, dramatizations to assist in history becoming alive, divide pupils up into doing committee work for peer mediated critical and creative thinking activities, among others. Observe off task behaviours to secure learner participation. Use of voice inflection guides pupils to be increasingly attentive. Active participation in learning improves sequence within the pupil (Guilfoyle, 2006).

- pupils must become motivated to attain ordered objectives within lessons and units of study. Increased energy levels are then available for pupils to devote to tasks being pursued. Social studies teachers must study each pupil's behaviour to notice that which motivates such as project methods, problem-solving experiences, reading/reporting on library books read, choice of activities at a learning center in the classroom, small group work, among others. Intrinsic motivation generally works best; however some pupils feel motivation through extrinsic means. With intrinsic motivation, pupils perceive purpose in learning. Reasons are sensed for participating in an ongoing activity or within a unit of study. The motivation then comes from within the pupil. Extrinsic motivation stresses the importance of external rewards being necessary to feel the need for learning. They may consist of inexpensive awards such as an inked, rubber stamp of a turkey during the month of November for each correct item, for example, in a workbook exercise. The ratio may be increased to one stamped response for every five correct items. Extrinsic motivation aids selected learners to achieve sequentially in a more optimal manner (Parsons, 2008).
- pupils need to learn what is relevant. With relevancy, learners feel that what is acquired is practical and

updated. A quality current events programme makes for discussing vital, every day happenings. Newscasts from radio and TV, news magazines and newspapers, along with the internet provide relevant items for discussion. The social studies teacher must be certain that pupils possess background information to benefit from the new learnings (Ediger, 2002).

- pupil self-selection of library books, directly related to the ongoing unit of study assists learners to sequence their very own experiences. They tend to choose books which are of interest and on their reading level. The library books need to be informational, but there are selected quality narrative reading materials which pique interests and are fictional, but also related to the unit being stressed. The writer has known several individuals with high interest and knowledge in history which was acquired through reading historical novels. When these books are read during class time in Sustained Silent Reading (SSR), pupils improve in word recognition skills and subject matter knowledge. Words not recognized while reading may be ascertained by using context clues our phonics. Learners may do most sequencing in reading library books on their very own. Ideas read may be brought into small group or classroom discussions as they relate to the concepts and generalizations being emphasized. When supervising university student teachers in the public schools, the writer has noticed in selected observations that pupils' ideas from library book reading were used as a basis for discussion rather than the basal textbook. Pupil enthusiasm and contributions indicated that this was an enjoyable experience. Here, pupils need to respect the ideas of others.

There are selected concepts which are salient to stress when sequence in learning is operationalized :

- **advance organizers :** They assist pupils to understand what is taught whereby the social studies teacher presents subject matter which assists pupils to attach meaning to that which follows in the lesson/unit of study. A stimulating and brief prerequisite experience then is follow by the implemented lesson plan.
- **metacognition :** This concept refers to thinking about thinking. Thus, pupils are aided to recall and think about what was taught, leading to higher levels of cognition including critical and creative thinking. These processes help pupils to order ideas in promoting sequential learnings.
- **self-efficacy :** With sequential learnings, pupils develop a repertoire of salient subject matter in ongoing social studies lessons and units of study. Confidence is then achieved in attaining vital concepts and generalizations. Building blocks from previous social studies encounters assist in achieving new objectives. Feelings of adequacy might well come about due to relating the new with previously acquired subject matter and skills.
- **success in learning :** Pupils tend to like the social studies when they feel positively toward teaching and learning situations. Success in achievement is poignant. With success, the motivation is there to increase opportunities for social studies learnings. The self concept should thrive. Feelings of failure accrue when the self concept becomes minimized. Learnings which are too complex make for negative feelings and frustration, whereas content which is too easy might make for feelings of boredom (Vygotsky, 1978).

REFERENCES

Dunn, Ross E. (2008), "The Two World Histories," *Social Education*, 72 (5), 257-263.

Ediger, Marlow (1998), *The Holy Land*. Kirksville, Missouri: Simpson Publishing Company.

Ediger, Marlow (2002), "Current Events in the Social Studies," *Edutracks*, 7(3), 14-15.

Ediger, Marlow (2007), *Teaching the Social Studies*. New Delhi, India: Discovery Publishing House.

Guifoyle, Christy (2006), NCLB : Is There Life Beyond Testing?" *Educational Leadership*, 64(3), 8-13.

National Council for the Social Studies (1997), *Curriculum Standards for the Social Studies*. Edison, New York : Whitehurst and Clark.

Parker, Walter C. (2001), *Social Studies in Elementary Education*. Upper Saddle River, New Jersey : Merrill, Prentice Hall.

Parsons, Seth A. (2008), "Providing Ail Students Aces to Self Regulated Learning," *The Reading Teacher*, 61 (1), 8-14.

Vygotsky, L S. (1978), *Mind in Society : The Development of Higher Psychological Processes*. Cambridge, Massachusetts: Harvard University Press.

Mentoring in Social Studies

6

Quality social studies instruction is salient for all pupils. What happens on the local, state, national, and international levels affect each person, Then too, social studies should emphasize good citizenship in school and in society. A knowledgeable person with needed skills to function well in relating to others is important. People possess different values, beliefs, and cultures which indicate that each person must be accepting of others and stress a caring society. The social studies mentor might well assist the teacher in improving the curriculum involving objectives, learning activities, and appraisal procedures in ongoing lessons and units of study.

Defining the Role of the Mentor

Mentors must be well versed in teaching the social studies as well as apply appropriate psychological principles in ongoing lessons and units of study. They need to be able to work effectively with each teacher, using quality human relations. Being uncaring, rude, and arrogant have no roles to play in teaching and learning situations. Cooperatively, the mentor and teacher need to identify problematic situations and work harmoniously in their solution(s). There are situations which hinder learner progress in the social studies. These must be pin-pointed and resolved to assist pupils to achieve more optimally :

1. *Pupils not understanding vital concepts and generalizations.* Here, the mentor and the teacher must analyze reasons for this occurring. A variety of developmental appropriate experiences need to be in the offing. These must be sequenced so that more optimal achievement does occur. The pace of lesson presentations should be such that acquisition of concepts and generalizations are attained with meaning theory being emphasized. Continual diagnosis need to be stressed so that learner achievement is in evidence (Wolk, 2008).
2. *Pupils need assistance in scaffolding.* When learnings appear to be too complex, within reason, the teacher perceives a gap between what the pupil is achieving and what might be possible To close the identified gap, a series of carefully ordered learnings may make for closure (Ediger, 2010).
3. *Pupils need to be engaged in ongoing lessons and units of study.* With involvement, pupils perceive interest in achieving salient objectives. The learner and the curriculum become one with the interest factor inherent in learning. There are fewer distractions and less lack of time on task, when each pupil is focused on the learning activity at hand. Disruptions in learning need to be replaced with interesting experiences in the social studies (Parsons, 2008).
4. pupils must feel that purpose is involved in pursuing, growing, and developing. Meaningless subject-matter consisting of facts and trivia must be replaced with vital concepts and generalizations. The mentor and the social studies teacher cooperatively need dialogue to come up with what is worthwhile and purposeful to the learner (Young and Gates, 2005).

5. *Pupil self-monitoring stresses the importance of learner ownership of the curriculum.* Thus, the pupil reflects upon what has been acquired and comes up with more accurate ideas in terms of subject-matter learnings.

The mentor is a guide and motivator in assisting each teacher to put forth maximum effort in teaching and learning situations. He/she does not dictate nor force selected behaviours upon the teacher, but rather intrinsically helps social studies teachers to analyze teaching behaviours with the intent of providing pupils with challenging, developmentally appropriate experiences. The mentor must be highly knowledgeable about different philosophies of instruction in order to provide the best fit for individual styles of learning. Mandated objectives are predetermined and measurably stated, for teachers to use in teaching and learning situations. These ends represent targets to aim toward in the instructional arena. Learning activities are aligned with the precise objectives. After instruction, the teacher may measure to ascertain if the specific objective(s) have been achieved. Generally, it is an either/or situation if the objective has been attained by the learner. There is little/no leeway in the interpretation of any objective. In contrast, constructivism stresses that the pupil sequences his/her own experiences. Thus, for example, in an ongoing social studies lesson, pupil(s) with teacher guidance identify a problem area. The problem is delimited so it can be solved. An hypothesis, or tentative answer, is developed. Learners then seek reference materials for possible solutions. A variety of relevant sources need to be used such as AV materials, knowledgeable resource personnel, internet and world wide web data, as well as traditional reading sources including reputable basal textbooks and library books. This provides ample opportunities to evaluate subject matter from the different sources of information to come up with an answer to the identified problem area. The hypothesis is then accepted, modified, or refuted. In the problem solving arena, the learner then sequences his/her own experiences. There are no specifically arranged objectives for pupil attainment along the spectrum. Instead, constructivism, represented here by problem solving, is holistic whereby there is a general framework, which is very open ended, leaving room for pupil initiative, creativity, and critical thought. At each ordered step along the way, the pupil with teacher assistance aids the pupil in the involved process toward completion. The pupil is responsible for quality work in problem solving and owns the curriculum together with the teacher. There is no lecture and no predetermined objectives; flexibility is involved in the learner following through on broad guidelines in problem solving. The mentor then must be highly educated in different philosophies of instruction including the use of measurable stated objectives versus constructivism with in-between points being possible (Ediger, 2010).

Many experts in social studies instruction praise the merits of small group learning as compared to individual endeavors. Here, learning style choices and preferences vary among pupils. The mentor and the social studies teacher need to evaluate which works best for learners. Perhaps, there must be rational balance between the two procedures due to individuals needing to work collectively as well as individually in school and in society. With either approach, the teacher needs to observe that all are on task and achieving (Kielsmeier, 2010).

REFERENCES

Ediger, Marlow (1999), *The Holy Land.* Kirksville, Missouri: Simpson Publishing Company.

Ediger, Marlow (2010), "Constructivism and the Social Studies," *Edutracks*, 9 (7), 13-14. Published in India.

Kielsmeier, James C. (2010), "Build a Bridge Between Service and Learning," *Phi Delta Kappan*, 91 (5), 8-15).

Parsons, Seth A. (2008), "Providing All Students with Access to Self Regulated Learning," *The Reading Teacher*, 61 (8), 628-635.

Wolk, S. (2008), "Joy in School," *Educational Leadership*, 66 (1), 8-14.

Young, Raymond, and Carl M. Gates (2005), "Playful Communication in Mentoring," *College Student Journal*, 39 (4), 692-701.

Portfolios in Social Studies

7

There are a plethora of ways to show pupil achievement in the social studies, one of which is the portfolio. Portfolio evaluation follows the thinking of constructivists who place major emphasis upon the pupil as an individual. Here, the pupil with teacher assistance is involved in selecting the entries. A Table of Contents provides structure for its contents. The portfolio is a flexible means of appraisal. Numerical results in terms of percentiles are not given in the assessment process. Instead, pupil progress may be viewed directly from authentic sources, such as products from the learner. A rubric may be utilized to appraise the portfolio and agreed upon standards used by evaluators to provide for interscorer reliability. The portfolio permits responsible observers to notice achievement as. well as what is left to learn.

There are numerous of kinds of products which may be placed into a social studies portfolio. Each entry reveals what has been emphasized in ongoing lessons and units of study.

Selecting Products for the Portfolio

The pupil with teacher guidance must carefully choose which representative products should become a part of the portfolio.

These products represent the work of a specific pupil and should not only satisfy the child but also communicate achievement. They indicate progress of dated entries and might well show sequentially how well a pupil is doing in school. The learner owns the portfolio and should feel pride in its accomplishments. The following entries, among others, need to be included with an accompanying Table of Contents showing the work of the child :

- electronic illustrations of art work, murals, construction items, and other projects completed in the social studies
- photos of committees, including the involved pupil, participating in problem-solving experiences.
- graphs (line, bar, circle), tables containing data from diverse units of study, charts developed (organizational, pedigree, narrative, classification), drawings made, time lines, and diagrams.
- videos of dramatics participation (creative, informal, and formal) in social studies units of study.
- recordings of oral book reports, debates, reader's theater, and committee endeavours.
- written summaries, outlines, poems written, and reports.

Each of the above portfolio entries may contribute much to successful parent/teacher conferences. By viewing and evaluating learner products, parents may assess authentic achievements. Questions may well be raised and discussions follow. Agreements might be made on specifics parents can help in to foster pupil progress. Reflection is necessary to notice additional assistance needed with learners, also, being actively involved in the evaluation process. This should motivate pupil progress. An effective social studies curriculum must meet the needs of pupils individually and collectively. Pupils differ from each other in myriad ways including abilities, interests, and attitudes. Thus, the teacher needs to consider a plethora of factors when assisting pupil learning in the social studies (Ediger, 2009).

Constructivism in the Social Studies

Constructivism, as a psychology of learning, emphasizes that pupils, individually, construct their very own knowledge and this is modified as ensuing lessons and units of study progress. Knowledge and skills then do not remain static, but are subject to change and modification. The teacher guides, motivates, and encourages learning, but does not dictate, lecture, or reprimand pupils to achieve. He/she facilitates learning. Self motivation by the pupil is salient and is assisted by others to grow, develop, and learn. Responsibility for learning rests upon the pupil. When the teacher notices pupils, in ongoing lessons and units of study, experience difficulties, he/she provides learnings to overcome problem areas. Thus, a teacher may not directly answer a pupil's question, but offer assistance on where to locate the needed information. Then too, the teacher might, in response to a pupil's question, raise related questions, leading the pupil to the necessary response. Inductive learning is heavily stressed whereby pupils learn by discovery. Learning is an active process. The teacher assists at the time a pupil faces a dilemma and this helps the learner to establish equilibrium, as well as move forward in achieving holism (Wolk, 2008).

Constructivism is somewhat opposite of behaviorism which is commonly stressed in the curriculum. Behaviourism emphasizes that objectives of instruction be established prior to instruction. The objectives can be clarified by having the teacher state what is expected of learners as a result of teaching. They are specific and leave little/no leeway for interpretation. Pupils then generally know what is expected of them. This provides security to learners. After instruction has occurred, the teacher may test pupils to notice if successful teaching has occurred and pupils have achieved stated objectives. Measurement is very important to behaviourists. For teacher written tests, the percent of correct answers is noticed. With state mandated testing, pupil's scores can be show with percentiles. For example, out of every one hundred pupils tested, 65 are below and 35 above for a learner who scored on the 65th percentile. Precision is involved with pupils either being correct/incorrect on multiple choice test items taken on a mandated test or for a teacher written test (Rose, 1999).

Behaviourism emphasizes that learning opportunities be aligned with the stated objectives so that pupils have a better chance at success. The teacher may then directly teach so that pupils achieve objectives and are successful in achieving. E. L. Thorndike in the early 1900s emphasized selected basic philosophical principles of behaviorism :

- whatever exists, exists in some amount.
- if it exists in some amount, it can be measured.

These beliefs brought the testing movement into vogue with tests being developed in a plethora of areas such as academic achievement in different curriculum areas, vocational skills, attitudes, personality development, among others. Measurement was a key concept here and in present day schools, testing is the rule rather than the exception. Tracking of pupil progress stresses the importance of viewing test scores over a period of time to notice progress over previous times of measurement, during the public school years. Is progress being made by the involved learner?

With computer use, mass numbers of pupil test results may be evaluated in a short period of time. These can be retrieved and shown readily on a monitor, for evaluation by teachers, principals, supervisors, superintendents of schools, as well as other responsible persons (Eddy *et al.*, 1997). There are questions to be raised pertaining to behaviorism as a psychology of learning :

- How appropriate is it to minimize pupil questions when emphasizing predetermined objectives of instruction?

The objectives then are stated prior to instruction and with aligned learning activities determine what is taught.

- With highly precise objectives, does teaching stress pupils learn specific facts which can be measured through multiple choice test items? Responses to multiple choice test items require exact answers with no leeway for pupil thought.
- Do teachers teach toward pupils doing well on tests rather than higher levels of cognition?
- With pupils zooming in on the correct answer, does this approach minimize creative thinking possibilities?

Test results can be incorporated into a portfolio, along with those mentioned above for constructivist psychology of instruction (Gardner, 1993).

REFERENCES

Eddy, John, *et al.* (1997), Technology Assisted Instruction, *Education*,117 (3), 478-480.

Ediger, Marlow (2009), "Supervising the Student Teacher in the Public School," *Education*, 130 (2), 251-254.

Gardner, Howard (1993), *Multiple Intelligences: Theory and Practice*. New York: Basic Books.

Rose, M. (1999), *"Ten Easy Writing Lessons That Get Kids Ready for Writing Assessments,"* New York; Scholastic.

Wolk, S. (2008), "Joy in School," *Educational Leadership*, 66 (1), 8-14.

8 Metacognition, Reading and Social Studies

A considerable amount of reading is generally emphasized in the social studies.This may cause problems, especially for those having difficulties in decoding. There is much the social studies teacher can do to assist pupils in reading comprehension. A repertoire of strategies need to be in the offing to aid pupils in developing meanings from print. Basal textbooks, accompanying workbooks, primary sources of information, the internet, among others, contain abstractions which need to be understandable in subject matter content. It is indeed frustrating for pupils to have reading assignments which lack meaning. Learners must be assisted to achieve as optimally as possible in all learning opportunities including reading in the social studies. What might be done to facilitate these kinds of activities?

Guidelines in Teaching

The teacher should always stress going from the known to the unknown in teaching/learning situations. Thus, illustrations, directly related to the lesson/unit being studied might well be utilized as a strategy in assisting pupils in reading. Each illustration needs elaboration which guides pupils to relate to the ensuing content. Pupils, also, need to predict what will transpire as a result of reading. Predictions may be recorded on the whiteboard; pupils may check to notice how closely the predictions came about. This assists pupils to focus upon the subject-matter content. Subsequently, ideas obtained may be discussed and integrated with predictions made. Reflection is emphasized with recalling previous knowledge as well as with related predictions. This makes it possible, too, to come up with creative ideas. Novel, unique thoughts are then in the offing. Relationship of knowledge is salient to stress in securing background information, prior to the ensuing reading activity, with possibilities to think of what might happen as the experience progresses (Ediger, 2009a&b).

Too frequently, pupils are not lead to reflect, thus making for shallowness in thinking. Indepth thought encourages, not only creative thinking, but also critical thought. The reader does not accept social studies content read as fact, but analyzes subject-matter into component categories. This allows specifics to be separated in terms of absolutes from tentativeness, imagination from reality, as well as fiction from non-fiction. Subject-matter then becomes more holistic when this separation and then integration has occurred. Ideas in the social studies are subject to change and are definitely not fixed and final (Ahmad, 2009). The inquiring mind perceives gaps in knowledge and seeks wholeness. Thus within the project method and unit of study, pupils with teacher guidance may decide, for example, upon a construction project related to a social studies unit on grain farming. This breathes reality and practicality into the social studies. Plans for the model need to be made including the following :

- crop rotation and possible terracing, e.g. wheat rotated with soybeans and terraces made on hilly land to minimize/avoid soil erosion
- storage bins on the farm to store grain, prior to its selling on the open market

- model self-propelled combines and tractors with air conditioned cabs
- large trucks or an eighteen wheeler which hauls the grain from the combine to the metal storage bins on the farm
- grain augurs which augur the grain from the truck into the storage bin.

In metacognition, pupils develop and focus upon broad and supporting ideas such as,

> "Farming methods have changed much in the last twenty years to include self-propelled combines which cut a forty foot wide swath in the wheat field at one time. All of the latest tractors and combines have air conditioned cabs. Farming is highly specialized with grain farms, dairy farms, cage layers for egg production, broilers (young chickens), or hog complexes. It is indeed rare for a farm to have more than one enterprise."

Metacognition then requires a large fund of developmental appropriate knowledge to go from the known to the unknown when reading. The knowledge provides background information to make the ensuing familiar when reading. Vocabulary study is important and must be stressed prior to and during reading, silently or orally. These new words may be printed in neat manuscript letters on the white board for all too see clearly. They should be discussed in terms of meaning and used in sentences, related to those to be read. Pupils must be taught to reflect upon these learnings and raise questions pertaining to what is not understood (Ediger, 2009a&b).

For needed word recognition techniques while reading, the pupil must reflect upon using context clues, phonics, as well as seeing smaller words within the larger word to make use of subject matter read. Dividing an unrecognized word into prefixes, suffixes, and root, also aids in reading holistically. He/she needs to attend to major generalizations and supporting details. This adds structure to main ideas acquired. Continually, the reader must pay attention to comprehension by reflecting upon what has been read. Retention, through reflection, is salient in reading (Parsons, 2008)!

Follow-up Learning Opportunities

Follow-up experiences should be open-ended, but include evaluating each prediction prior to reading. These should be assessed in an atmosphere of respect. Ridicule, rudeness, and feelings of haughtiness have no role to play in a quality social studies program. Developing good citizens becomes a major objective. Civility is often lacking in the media, in school, and in society, making it necessary for schools to modify and remediate these behaviors. Questions raised by pupils need exploration and answers found. Here, problem solving, as an extended learning activity, becomes important. Thus, a relevant problem by pupils is identified within an ongoing unit of study. The problem needs to be delimited so that it is capable of being solved. An hypothesis is developed with a variety of reference sources used to secure necessary information. Deliberation, thought, and effort go into problem solving activities. Information obtained is evaluated in terms of accuracy, completeness, as well as being vital. This makes it possible to modify, refute, or accept the original hypothesis. Problem solving may be individual or within a committee setting. If collective work is stressed, ideas circulate within the committee members and are freely discussed with the intent of finding the best solution. Solutions to problems need to be shared within the classroom as well as with others. School newsletters sent home may include items of interest such as problem solving and project methods of study, among others in the total curriculum. Quality communication between home and school assists in working together for the good of the learner. Parents need to be invited to visit school and see social studies displays and activities. They might well reflect upon how to optimize achievement in knowledge, skills, and attitudes (Cooper, 2009).

Electronic photos of student work in the social studies may displayed on bulletin board settings as well as outside the classroom hall. Pupil pride in accomplishments provide ample opportunities for metacognitive reflection. Metacognition then provides situations whereby evaluation of achievement occurs. Thus, the learner appraises how well something was attained as well as ways to improve learnings. Gaps in learning, too, are perceived with the end result being to acquire what is lacking. Curiosity in desiring to achieve results in doing extra credit work as in developing a book report or chart (narrative, classification, organizational, and/or agricultural products), related to a topic in an ongoing lesson/unit of study. Reading experiences should extend learnings whereby the learner relates content read to the self, to other texts and topics, and to others in society. Relationship of knowledge, ideas, and abilities makes for holism in learning (Bonds-Raacke and Raacke, 2008).

Portfolios and Evaluation in the Social Studies

A major approach in assessing pupil progress might well be a portfolio procedure. Here, the pupil with teacher guidance collects products of his/her work and develops a portfolio of vital accomplishments. A representative sampling of dated entires is then placed into the portfolio. A table of contents gives order to the entries of a pupil which include :

- diagrams, charts, illustrations, tables and graphs, as well as maps
- summaries, reports, outlines, and letters
- electronic photos of construction activities, art activities, projects, murals, models made, committees at work, and relief maps developed
- recordings of oral communication experiences (Vygotsky, 1978).

Contents in the portfolio provide ample opportunities for reflection and sharing with parents of the involved pupil.

Here, the pupil as well as the teacher may describe progress in terms of the dated entries. Actual products are observed and not test scores only. Observers may evaluate what is done well as well as what needs improvement. Diagnosis and remediation are then inherent. Self-evaluation by the pupil is stressed, with a reflective emphasis. Then too, the pupil is engaged in oral communication between a sender and a receiver. Active pupil engagement, interest, and purpose are salient factors in the evaluation process.

Additional assessment procedures to use are valid and reliable teacher written tests, learner participation in discussions, as well as observation of attitudes and feelings. However, the emphasis should be placed upon what the learner knows and does in everyday course work.

REFERENCES

Ahmad, Sajjad (2009), "Evolving a Framework for Teaching and Learning," *Edutracks*, 8(9), 11-12.

Bonds-Raacke, Jennifer, and John D. Raacke (2008), Using Table PCs in the Classroom : An Investigation of Student's Expectations and Reactions," *Journal of Instructional Psychology*, 35 (3), 235-239.

Cooper, Patricia M. (2009), "Children" Literature for Reading Strategy-Instruction, Innovation, or Interference?, *Language Arts*, 86 (3), 178-187.

Ediger, Marlow (2009a), "Supervising the Student Teacher in the Public School," *Education*, 130 (2), 251-254.

Ediger, Marlow (2009b), "Seven Criteria for an Effective Classroom Environment," *College Student Journal*, 43 (4), 1370-1372.

Parsons, Seth (2008), "Providing all Students Access to Self Regulated Literacy Learning," *The The Reading Teacher*, 61 (8), 628-636.

Vygotsky, L. S. (1978), Mind in Society : *The Development of Higher Psychological Processes*. Cambridge, Massachusetts : Harvard University Press.

9 Leadership in Social Studies Curriculum

Selected forms of inservice education are costly or moderately expensive. The writer observed an inservice social studies education programme which was definitely inexpensive and yet participants seemingly gained much from its offering. Once participants were initially engaged, motivation was high! The social studies teachers involved in the inservice programme had access to a professionals library consisting of educational journals, social studies teaching periodicals, video tapes on classroom practices, as well as recent university level teacher education textbooks. Informally, teachers had discussed changes which needed to be made in the instructional arena, but this had never gone beyond the talking stage. A more organized procedure would benefit teachers in the social studies. Thus, involved teachers met for the first time in an informal setting, discussing what they would like to know more about and the possibility of implementing innovative procedures. The feeling, among other factors, was that pupils forgot too much of what had been learned. Was there a way to assist increased retention of what had been taught?

Metacognition and the Social Studies

One concept which these teachers wished to learn more about

was metacoqnition. Would retention increase if pupils engaged in metacognition strategies? In retrospect, teachers analyzed how much of metacognition was used to reflect upon previous lessons taught. They marveled at how little was recalled. After researching articles from educational literature in the school's professional library on metacognition, a conscious effort was placed upon reflection. This was discussed indepth in the inservice group of social studies teachers. In subsequent meetings, teachers truly recalled more of what was taught and what went awry. They also assisted pupils in metacognitive strategies, which seemingly lead to improved concentration and retention.

With metacognition, teachers felt that this concept was salient, not only in teaching, but also in every day happenings. Improved efforts resulted in decisions made. Both teachers and pupils reflected more about learnings attained in the social studies. The teachers felt that a higher quality of teaching resulted. The following, among others, received more emphasis :

- pupils, due to self evaluation, identified which concepts and generalizations needed more attention
- teachers were more careful, than previously, in evaluating materials of instruction used as learning activities, based on their previous experiences
- increased attention was given to critical and creative thinking rather than covering subject matter in a textbook
- teachers were more discerning in terms of what works to secure learner achievement.

Social studies teachers were more motivated in teaching as well as discerning in choosing objectives, learning experiences for pupils to attain objectives, and assessment techniques. Explicit instruction as well as situated learning were used, among other procedures, in teaching. Teachers experimented with metacognition strategies in the classroom and reported back to the inservice group. Video taped teaching, observed by the inservice group, assisted in analyzing what had transpired in teaching. Where was reflection emphasized? What revelations were there which assisted pupil retention involving metacognition? An enthused set of teachers engaged in critical and creative thinking in discussing these video tapes.

Multiple Intelligences Theory in Teaching

These social studies teachers were interested in a multiplicity of procedures in improving the curriculum. They explored numerous options in the instructional arenas. Along with metacognition strategies, they showed much interest in pursuing multiple intelligences theory in integrating the social studies. Teachers elaborated on talents and abilities observed of pupils and how these may be utilized to enhance social studies teaching. The following intelligences were pursued by teachers in inservice education :

- **spatial :** Here, the discussion centered upon using art activities in an integrated curriculum. Might art assist pupils in liking ongoing lessons and units where their individual intelligence may be used? This lead to art experiences and ways this intelligence may be used strategically in a lesson.
- **logic as used in mathematics teaching :** Here, participants delved into pupils thinking logically in the social studies. It was agreed upon that logical thinking needs emphasis. Specific examples were mentioned situationally to clarify thinking with teachers volunteering to try out this intelligence in teaching the social studies.
- **objective thought as in science :** The stress here was upon separating facts from opinions, as well as fantasy from reality, in ongoing lessons and units of study.
- **manual dexterity with a hands on approach in pupil learning :** Several teachers exclaimed that they always

had pupils in the classroom who excelled in learning with a hands on approach.

- **verbal intelligence as in reading and writing activities :** This is the favourite approach in learning for selected pupils. These learners accomplish much in acquiring relevant concepts and generalizations from decoding and encoding experiences in reading social studies content. They might well serve as models for others in the classroom. Cooperative learning might be enhanced when a good reader is in the group for problem solving experiences. However, others need to do their fair share of committee endeavor work. Careful evaluation by the teacher is needed to help all in cooperative endeavors to learn, do well and not lean upon the good readers only in data gathering. In writing up the findings, the inservice group felt that careful assessment is needed to monitor how well each helped in the final writeup. The inservice ed group felt that adequate attention in terms of time was given here, but pupils seemingly did not benefit as optimally as they should especially from reading in the social studies. Careful listening and accurate communication of ideas in a group setting needed further emphasis.
- learning styles such as pupils working in small groups as compared to individual endeavours. Teachers, here, reflected upon situations whereby high quality work was done by all members of a committee and also where one committee member did all of the work; the others were content with getting a good grade for the total committee contributions, but they had sat by idly. There also were pupils who excelled when working by the self. A lively discussion followed whereby both sides of the coin were debated.

Ultimately, a balance between small group and individual achievement was advocated. But, the research would continue between cooperative versus individual emphasis in social studies instruction.

Scaffolding Learner Achievement

Scaffolding provided an interesting concept for social studies teachers to study. The question arose among teachers, "How do we get pupils to attain more complex generalizations, and yet not frustrate learning?" By securing indepth information on scaffolding, several teachers volunteered to implement this concept in teaching and report back at the committee's subsequent meeting. This was especially useful in teaching social studies vocabulary. For example, in teaching economic concepts such as consumption, pupils were asked what they consumed in school as in food items in the lunch room. By making the abstract concept "consumption" concrete, pupils readily attached meaning to that term. Many examples of scaffolding were mentioned by teachers who, in turn, implemented the use of this concept. Scaffolding may be emphasized in the following situations :

- asking questions of learners when they feel frustrated at a given point, and these lead pupils to subsequent answers whereby success in learning is observed
- meaningfully assist pupils in problem solving in demonstrating how to secure needed information when guiding pupils to test an hypothesis
- showing pupils, sequentially, how to proceed in planning a social studies project
- helping pupils write up a plan to accompany their construction project for the social studies fair.

The Interest Factor in Learning

A major problem identified by inservice education participants was how to secure as well as maintain pupil interest in ongoing lessons and units of study. If pupils accepted the interest factor in ongoing lessons and units of study, there would, perhaps, be little lost time in achieving objectives of instruction. Participants mentioned during the discussion points of pupil interest observed. They also discussed where interest had been lacking. Their concern pertained to learners acquiring interest in whatever was being pursued in the social studies. The inservice teachers began with initiating a new unit in developing pupil interest. What kinds of initiating experiences would then capture learner attention?

After more research had been done from the teacher's library, they analyzed broad guidelines read as well as specific kinds of learning experiences. It seemingly was up to the teacher to try out different activities which might possibly entice pupil learning. The following guidelines were summarized to encourage learning involving interest :

- pupils need to understand and not merely memorize subject-matter.
- learners need to have a voice in determining objectives, learning activities, and appraisal procedures.
- learnings presented deductively or acquired inductively must adhere to appropriate order.
- self-evaluation by pupils is important and not only from test results.
- a variety of approaches in evaluation must be used in appraising pupil performance including portfolios, dramatic experiences, written work such as book reports and engaging in outlining of content.
- learning experiences need to be adapted to having pupils achieve as optimally as possible.
- objectives of instruction, in selected situations, need to be negotiated between pupils and teachers.

Energized social studies teachers felt that by studying and using innovative ideas in the classroom such as concepts emphasized above, pupils achieved more and teachers also felt that it was motivating to observe pupil retention increase. Inservice education approaches should be based upon assisting pupils to achieve, grow, and develop. Then too, use can be made of learnings acquired. It is not inservice education for the sake of doing so, but rather knowledge and skills acquired are practical and utilitarian. These social studies teachers felt that time allotted to studying in-depth what pupils need in terms of assistance in learning is time well spent. It was indeed motivating to feel efficacious in utilizing methodology which works, according to a social studies teacher. It takes knowledge of these methods, but also skill in putting them to use. The self concept of teachers improved as a result of learnings acquired. Social studies teacher efficacy is salient in being able to assist each pupil to progress more optimally.

Meeting Esteem Needs of Pupils in Social Studies

10

Pupils need to attain as optimally as possible in the curriculum, social studies being no exception. Learners, presently, will be citizens of tomorrow and social studies learnings must make its many contributions. Thus, social studies teachers need to choose objectives with deliberation and thought, select appropriate learning opportunities to achieve these objectives, and emphasize evaluation procedures which are valid and reliable to appraise learner progress.

Holistic development of the learner is of utmost importance. The physical, emotional, social, and intellectual development of learners need integration into each unit of study.

Teaching and Learning in the Social Studies

A major objective in meeting esteem needs is to develop pupils' feelings of success in learning. Here, pupils interact with appropriate learning experiences and accomplish personal goals. Interest in learning assists pupils to put forth effort in achieving knowledge in history, geography, economics, political science, and anthropology/sociology. The social studies teacher must be well acquainted with each pupil in terms of background knowledge and skills possessed before launching a new unit of study. He/she takes a personal interest in each learner and listens carefully to subject matter pupils present in ongoing discussions. It is good for the teacher to keep anecdotal records of pupils where dated entries are made to keep track of what pupils know and have left to learn. In this way, the social studies teacher may build upon previous learnings acquired by pupils. New objectives then to be acquired provide for improved sequence in ongoing learning activities. Success in learning builds confidence in the self with esteem needs being met (Ediger, 2007).

Second, pupils need to be rewarded for achievement in the curriculum. Verbal praise for quality progress made builds morale for learning. Pupils have an inward desire to feel a need for being rewarded for accomplishments. To go to school each day and feel that learning is not rewarded makes for a lack of motivation. Pupils individually as well as in committees must feel they are achieving well and this comes to fruition when a verbal reward is forthcoming.

Third, pupil interest is a powerful factor in achievement. Learning may be intrinsically motivating when there is a thirst for knowledge and skills in ongoing social studies units. When facts, concepts, and generalizations become interesting to pupils; pupil motivation comes from within to accomplish, achieve, and grow. With interest in ongoing social studies units of study, pupils inwardly reach out for new knowledge and skills. The teacher's role here is to choose learning opportunities which capture and nurture. He/she needs to observe pupils if active active engagement in learning is forthcoming. Involvement in tasks, duties, and responsibilities in each lesson taught should capture learner interests. The learner and the social studies become one and not separated from each other. Interest in learning propels pupils to put forth effort in attaining vital personal goals in the curriculum. Intrinsically with interest, esteem needs are being met with an inward desire for acquiring further knowledge and skills (Parker, 2001).

Fourth, a quality classroom climate invites pupils to interact positively with others and with different materials of instruction. Cooperative endeavours, as a result, become satisfying as a means of goal attainment. A good learning atmosphere then emphasizes the following :

- respect and acceptance of others in the school setting.
- feelings of caring and wanting to assist others, as needed.
- positive attitudes with no leeway for rudeness, harassment, ill-will, and retribution.
- freedom to move around to secure needed materials and supplies as well as to interact with others.
- acceptance of ideas expressed and not interrupting others when communicating content within a committee setting (Ediger, 2009).

With satisfying small group work, there is assistance for pupils in developing self esteem. Too frequently, learning opportunities are boring and fail to challenge the individual or group. With experiences which promote happiness in ongoing tasks, the pupil tends to feel good about the self and motivates achievement and learning.

Fifth, self-efficacy is promoted with indepth acquisition of relevant subject matter. Improved preparation from rich past experiences helps pupils to tackle increasingly complex ideas in the social studies. Quality work in completing assignments and volunteering to complete additional activities should make the pupil increasingly proficient in the different academic branches of the social sciences. Integration of content here provides information for indepth problem solving in which there is a problem, hypothesis, and means of testing the hypothesis. Problem solving might well be emphasized as an enrichment a activity as well as within an ongoing unit of study. Self efficacy or motivated efforts to achieve whereby the pupil feels confidence in learning is salient (Ray, 2006).

Sixth, reflection upon previous experiences builds confidence in reviewing major concepts and generalizations in noticing their accuracy as well as completeness. If inaccuracies or incompleteness are noted through reflection, the pupil may pursue individual experiences to take care of deficiencies noted. A concern exists for wholeness in pursuing social studies knowledge and skills. Esteem needs are met in desiring correctness in the academics.

Seventh, purposeful learning experiences are important. If a pupil perceives purpose or reasons for learning, then reasons for making progress should abound. To frequently, assignments are made in the social studies with no accompanying reasons being provided for their completion. The learner needs to be motivated to perceive inherent reasons. He/she feels energized when perceived purpose is accepted by the pupil. If, for example, the pupil is a participant in a social studies fair, then a purpose will be to do well in completing a project and

- providing reasons for engaging in this experience
- indicating plans for doing the project
- stating the criteria for its evaluation.

A social studies fair where projects are judged in terms of quality as well as in daily work in the classroom, pupils can have esteem needs met. This is certainly a possibility for all pupils!

REFERENCES

Ediger, Marlow (2007), "Teacher Observation to Assess Student Achievement," *Journal of Instructional Psychology,"* 34 (2), 137-139.

Ediger, Marlow (2009), "The Principal in the Teaching and Learning Process," *Education*, 129 (4), 574-578.

Parker, Walter C. (2001), *Social Studies in Elementary Education*, Upper Saddle River, New Jersey: Prentice-Hall, Inc.

Ray, Katie Wood (2006), "What Are You Thinking?" *Educational Leadership*, 64 (2), 58-62.

Recent Trends in Teaching Social Studies

11

Teachers, Supervisors and School Administrators need to stay abreast of and implement selected trends in teaching the social studies. Pupils in cla1ssrooms then need to attain updated objectives of instruction, learning activities to achieve the objectives, and evaluation procedures to analyze and notice pupil progress. The curriculum needs to be designed to reflect vital trends (Fitzhugh, 2006).

Trends as Guidelines to Design the Social Studies

These trends provide for a viable curriculum when being studied and implemented. Careful analyzation is necessary in order for the teacher to attach meaning to and determine the worth of each trend. Which trends then are salient in the social studies?

First, pupils need to acquire relevant subject-matter from the social sciences, which includes history (a study of vital main, subordinate ideas of the past and how they have influenced human beings), geography (the natural environment and its influence on human behavior), economics (purchasing and selling goods and services), political science (laws, rules, regulations, and how they affect human beings), and anthropology/sociology (culture and its affect on human behaviour). Key ideas and core concepts need identification and taught inductively as well as deductively, through explanations. These are incorporated into learning opportunities to assist pupils in attaining relevant objectives of instruction (Parker, 2001).

Second, a multi-media approach must be used in teaching and learning situations in order to provide for individual differences. Concrete (actual items and objects), semi-concrete (illustrations, charts, drawings, picture library books, power point presentations, video-tapes, resource personnel, among others,), and abstract materials (textbooks, encyclopaedias, the internet, world wide web, current events magazines, among others), provide subject matter for pupil acquisition. These materials may then be used as learning activities by adapting each to the present achievement levels of learners. They may be used as initiating activities, developmental experiences, or culminating experiences in ongoing units of study (Ediger, 2009).

Third, a variety of methods of instruction need to be used in meeting individual needs of learners. To meet these needs, pupils may experience the following :

- problem-solving whereby an hypothesis is developed in answer to a question. The hypothesis emphasizes deliberation and is tentative, subject to evaluation and modification.
- project methods in which a unit related construction activity is planned, completed, and evaluated.
- textbook methods whereby readiness for its reading is developed through viewing related illustrations, discussing new vocabulary terms, and identifying questions. Followup experiences include discussing subject matter read, and making use of its content such as dramatizing major ideas read, summarizing, drawing related illustrations, developing a chart, and/or making a model.

- inductive procedures in which pupils achieve generalizations through a learning by discovery procedure.
- deductive approaches in which pupils apply generalizations to a new situation.
- small group methods in which each pupil has opportunities to have input into a discussion in an atmosphere of respect toward others.
- large group sessions whereby pupils are introduced to a new lesson with the use of an AV aid.
- individual methods in which the learner pursues a purposeful activity on his/her own in the social studie.
- an art experience which relates directly to the ongoing lesson presentation.
- research opportunity whereby the pupil pursues and writes up information dealing with a vital topic (Ediger, 2008a).

Providing for each learner is important in order to extend and provide indepth experiences. The needs of the individual must be met so that present and future abilities of pupils have chances of growing, developing, and achieving.

Fourth, pupils need to have decision making responsibilities in school and in society. To make choices, from among alternatives, provides realistic experiences for pupils. Thus, in school and in the societal arenas, the pupil, may be bombarded with choices which need to be made :

- What to do in one's spare time
- How to proceed in making a model in the social studies
- Which topic to select to write about in an ongoing lesson
- How to divide up responsibilities in doing a group project.

Being able to plan well where cooperation is involved may become a part of every person's responsibilities throughout one's lifetime. Being a cordial participant and working together harmoniously with others is salient in making progress in goal attainment. There are social studies teachers who have developed several learning centers in a classroom. Pupils may select which tasks to complete from these centers. Decision making is involved. The choices to be made involve the following, among others :

- completing an individual or committee activity
- doing an art, a reading/writing, or construction project
- choosing committee members to work with (Ediger, 2008b).

The above lists a few of the many choices which need to be made in a learning centers approach in the teaching of the social studies. Being involved in small group work is essential presently as well as in future citizenship endeavours.

Fifth, quality sequence in learning makes for more optimal achievement. The social studies teacher must think in terms of ordered learnings for pupils. Thus, what is taught must be related to the immediate past experiences of learners. The present and past experiences of pupils need to be related, not isolated from each other. Thus, pupils may be assisted to develop their own knowledge and skills, known as constructionist psychology. As the discussion continues, the teacher helps pupils to attach understanding to that concept by raising questions pertaining to its meaning. The teacher does not tell its meaning but assists pupils to discover a definition. This is opposite of lecture whereby the teacher would provide its exact contextual definition. Constructivism stresses that the social studies teacher helps pupils to discover knowledge as sequential learnings are found. With lecture, the teacher determines subsequent learnings for pupils each step along the way. Thus with unknown words, the teacher determines how to define each, hoping the learner will understand what is taught. Here, the communication is a one way street in that subject matter moves from the communicator (the teacher) to the communicatee which is the pupil (Beer, *et al.*, 2008).

Sixth, a good current events program needs to be in the offing. Thus, separate sections on the bulletin board should be devoted to news clips and each discussed pertaining to :

- local news such as salient happenings on the local scene
- happenings and news on the state level including election for state officers
- news on the national level including campaigns for and election of officials on the national level, and budgetary items, among others
- world happenings including wars, trade among nations, and unemployment data.

Each news item needs thorough discussion and extended to other vital relationships. A democracy depends upon a well informed citizenry (Keefe, 2007).

Seventh, a quality evaluation programme must be in the offing to ascertain learner achievement and progress. The evaluation methods must be valid in that it measures what it purports to measure. Thus if the evaluation items measure problem-solving skills, it must do so, and not measure something else such as capitol cities of respective nations. Then too, the evaluation methods must emphasize reliability. Thus, consistency of results for a pupils are important in the evaluation dimension, For example, if a pupil ranks on the thirtieth percentile the first time a test is taken, and on the eightieth percentile on the same test taken the second time, the question arises, "What is the pupil's test results when they vary much from the thirtieth to the eightieth percentile on the same test?" Reliability is certainly lacking. Upon examination of the print out of pupil test results, the following might be noticed :

- some of the test items lacked clarity in writing due to vagueness in content.
- the vocabulary in test writing was not appropriate for the pupils' stage of development and maturity.

- the test items did not cover what was taught, indicating a lack of validity.
- the test items were not proofed carefully. Omitting a comma, for example, can make for much difference in item interpretation.
- there were too many interpretations of a test item's meaning.
- more than one correct response was possible, but this was not stated in the directions for test taking (Bracey, 2008).

Recognized standardized tests are pilot tested to take out poorly written test items. The print out from these studies provide the best developers with information on weak test items. These may then be revised. By having test takers take the same test over again, data is secured on test/retest reliability. Most teachers do not do this; perhaps this is due to a lack of time. But, all teachers may use the split/half method to determine reliability. Here, the test is given one time. The odd numbered items are then compared with the even numbered test items. Do those who score highest on the odd numbered items score in a similar manner on the even numbered test items? The computer then may provide a reliability figure in comparing the responses for odd versus even numbered test items. If the test is short in length, the teacher might scan to notice how the two compare with each other. Teachers should become highly knowledgeable about statistics due to information on validity, reliability, percentiles, standard deviations, among others.

On teacher developed tests, the writer has not mentioned anything about ascertaining validity. Here, the test writer may use face validity. Thus, directly after teaching, the teacher writes test items to cover what was taught. Validity, here, emphasizes that what was taught is transfered to one or more multiple choice test items. Then too, the stem and each of the four distractors must be grammatically correct as well as plausible. Plausibility states that there are no ridiculous responses; each is rational and makes sense as a distractor.

Teacher observation might well be a highly useful evaluation technique, providing that quality standards are used here. The social studies teacher may then appraise the following :

- pupil time on task
- resilience of the learner
- motivation to achieve
- harmoniously working together with others
- curiosity in subject matter as well as in environmental learnings
- respect for others.

Each of the above provides data for assisting pupils to achieve. Analysis and remediation might then well provide for sequential learning.

IN CLOSING

There are selected trends which social studies teachers need to follow. These trends provide a social studies programme for pupils which is of high quality as well as being relevant. The best of objectives, learning opportunities to achieve the objectives, as well as appraisal techniques, must be used as tools to optimize learner achievement and progress in the social studies.

REFERENCES

Beer *et al.* (2008), "Summer Learning Camps: Helping Students Prepare for College," *College Student Journal*, 42 (3), 930-938.

Bracey, Gerald B. (2008), "Research, The Algebra Hoax," Phi Delta Kappa, 90 (4), 306-307. Mr. Bracey writes highly informative items on research in each issue of the *Phi Delta Kappan*.

Ediger, Marlow (2009), "Scope in the Social Studies," *Edutracks*, 8 (6), 14-16.

Ediger, Marlow (2008a), "Leadership in the School Setting," *Education*, 129(1),17-20.

Ediger, Marlow (2008b), "The School and Students in Society," *Journal of Instructional Psychology*, 35 (3), 261-263.

Fitzhugh, Will (2006), "Where's the Content?" *Educational Leadership*, 64 (2), 42-47.

Keefe, James W. (2007), "What is Personalization?" *Phi Delta Kappan*, 217-224.

Parker, Walter C. (2001). *Social Studies in Elementary Education.* Upper Saddle River, New Jersey : Prentice-Hall, Inc.

Rating Teachers of Social Studies Instruction 12

Teachers are being increasingly held accountable for their quality of student instruction. They need to prepare well for each lesson taught and provide for individual differences among learners. Documentation of teaching success is desired. Tracking results of teacher effectiveness is salient. Thus, there needs to be an effective approach to use in noticing how well each teacher is doing in time.

Quality of Criteria in Rating

Standards used in the rating process must be carefully chosen with heavy involvement of teachers, supervisors, and school administrators. They need careful research, scrutiny, and study, prior to implementation. Social studies is a highly important academic discipline and needs to be included in any mandated system of testing to indicate its saliency. There are a plethora of reasons to be given for the importance of the social studies. A major reason being that threats to humanity exist if nations continually spend excessive amount of money on the military as well as plan attacks against each other. Deaths, destruction, and wounded individuals result. Post traumatic stress is commonly discussed and this involves traumas veterans experience from actual fighting in wars. Ways need to be found to minimize/eliminate militaristic fervor among inhabitants of any nation.

There are a plethora of ways to spend moneys to benefit humanity such as quality, affordable health care. Too may people go bankrupt when a costly malady hits a family. Then to moneys may be spent on improving infrastructure of an area such as safe roads, bridges, flood control projects, and safety in cities. Crime is rampant in certain areas where hostile gangs operate. More police and fire protection is necessary, the latter is indicated with the many cases of arson occurring.

Corruption in corporations is very costly to society with extremely high salaries paid to CEOs and board members, even with a failing economic operation. In addition stock options, and bonuses add to these unfortunate ventures. Morality and ethics are certainly a problem and a major one at that.

Thus, there are numerous reasons which might well be given to stressing strong social studies curricula in the public schools. This must include economic development, a democratic society, achievements in medical science, accomplishments in the fine arts and in architecture, as well as high productivity in agriculture, among others. Social studies teachers must provide leadership to emphasize quality in the curriculum. Quality may come from well prepared teachers, continual inservice education, adequate and purposeful teaching materials of instruction, support from school administrators and curriculum directors, and cooperating parents (Ediger, 2009). The question then arises, "How should social studies teachers be appraised?"

First, social studies teachers must become efficacious in that they are highly knowledgeable and confident in their chosen profession. They possess not only the knowledge but also needed methodology to provide for individual differences among pupils. Pupils are the focal point of attention. They must do the learning and be assisted to attain optimally in the social studies. Thus, pupils need to achieve well in subject matter, in skills, and in attitudes (Ediger, 2008).

Second, developing good citizens should be at the heart of teaching and learning situations. The social studies teacher needs to serve as a model. He/she needs to take an active role in societal responsibilities, exemplify good human relations, manage personal finances effectively, and develop a good self concept. The social studies teacher guides pupils to be very knowledgeable about being/implementing standards of being a good citizen. This is more than passing tests, which is important, but also there needs to be the desire to improve society for the benefit of all (Smith and Lambert, 2008).

Third, achieving advanced university degrees in the social sciences assists in developing leadership qualities to improve in the teaching of the social studies. The social studies teacher must experience quality course work in history, geography, economics, political science, anthropology/sociology, and psychology. What is studied on the university level needs to become a salient part of instruction in the public school setting. Teacher preparation programs in schools of education then should not be separated from actual public school teaching/learning situations. Connections must be made (Petress, 2006).

Fourth, lesson and unit construction must be designed to meet cognitive, affective, and psychomotor needs of pupils. Incorporated in each must stress the following psychological principles of learning :

- engagement of each learner in ongoing learning activities
- purposeful experiences whereby pupils perceive reasons for achieving
- provisions made for multiple intelligences in the classroom as well as styles of learning
- meaning and understanding emphasized

- challenge and success for learners inherent in planning for instruction (See Phillips, 2008).

By integrating the above named principles of learning in ongoing instruction, pupils should achieve more optimally in the social studies.

Fifth, classroom standards of conduct should be developed cooperatively involving the social studies teacher and learners. Reasons for these standards are to enhance learning and not for the sake of their development. The classroom environment should be such that pupils can achieve objectives in a satisfactory manner. This means that the classroom environment :

- stresses a business like atmosphere for learning
- politeness for all is in evidence. This must be true for teachers as well as pupils.

Sixth, acceptance of others is vital regardless of cultural backgrounds including religion, nationality, languages spoken, and native customs, among others. Too frequently, pupils are shunned who come from a primary group or another nation. If all are to attain more optimally, they need to develop feelings of belonging. Democracy as a way of life indicates that all are equal before the law, and therefore each person needs to possess feelings of equality of opportunity in human relations as well as in classroom endeavors. Learning opportunities need to emphasize this importance when provisions are made for individual differences in the classroom. Pupils come to the classroom with different interests, talents, and hobbies. Feelings of acceptance occur when esteem needs are met of learners. Pupils individually may not be rewarded for contributions made. Thus, esteem needs fail to be met of pupils, individually. All have something valuable to contribute including English Language Learners (ELL), slow learners, as well as those who are mainstreamed.

Seventh, integrated subject matter from the academic disciplines must be emphasized. In any social studies unit of study, the teacher may plan to integrate content to assist pupils to achieve well and to see connectedness. Content perceived as being related will be remembered longer than if perceived as isolated facts. For example, the following unit of study on Japan in terms of each academic discipline indicates the possibility of perceived relationships :

- the history of relevant concepts and generalizations to be stressed.
- geographical features comprising islands which makeup the nation of Japan.
- economic development which has aided Japan in becoming a leading industrial nation.
- the system and organization of government (political science).
- the music, art, architecture, foods eaten, music, level of technology, and culture of Japan.

The social studies teacher needs to relate academic disciplines where it is feasible and good to do so. The curriculum must be adapted to the present achievement levels of pupils. Continuous progress of learners is then achieved sequentially. Indepth teaching is recommended of major concepts and generalizations. A variety of materials of instruction must be used to capture and maintain pupil interest such as :

- concrete objects including models and objects of Japan
- semi-concrete materials including video tapes, power point presentations, illustrations, and pictures
- abstract print materials such as basal textbooks, library books, resource personnel, as well as computerized programs (Balathy, 2007).

IN CLOSING

Criteria were discussed pertaining to appraising social studies teachers. These are flexible criteria and may be written more concisely to use in ratings given by responsible persons (students, teachers, and school administrators) to social studies teachers. Feedback needs to be given to assist in developing quality teachers of the social studies.

REFERENCES

Balathy, Ernest (2007), "Technology and Current Reading/Literacy Assessment Strategies," *Reading Teacher*, 61 (3), 240-248.

Ediger, Mariow (2008), "Current Events in the Social Studies," *Social Studies Review*, 47 (2), 58-60.

Ediger, Mariow (2009) "Scope in the Social Studies," *Edutracks*, 8 (6), 14-16.

Petress, Ken (2006), "An Operational Definition of Class Participation," *College Student Journal*, 40 (4), 821-823.

Phillips, Antoinette, et.al. (2008), "Enhancing a Curriculum: A Focus on the Developmental Process," *College Student Journal*, 42 (4), 1070-1074.

Smith, Rick, and Mary Lambert (2008), "Assuming the Best," *Educational Leadership*, 66 (1), 16-21.

13 Student Teacher and Social Studies

What kind of experiences in the teaching of the social studies sequence would best equip the future teacher to do well as a professional? The pre-service university curriculum should stress that which assists the student teacher to secure a repertoire of quality experiences in the teaching of the social studies. A highly knowledgeable student teacher of the social sciences, possessing skill in teaching pupils, should aid learners in the public schools to possess subject matter knowledge and social skills to do well in society (Ediger, 2008a&b).

Undergraduate Sequence

The pre-service teacher needs to have a general education background which prepares the individual in becoming proficient as a regular teacher. Too frequently, the pre-service program is separated from teaching and learning situations in the public schools. Rather, it should become integrated. Thus, freshmen English classes need to stress ingredients making for quality writing. Much written work indicative of diverse purposes in writing must be in the offing. For example, in writing an essay, the following need emphasis in actual writing experiences :

- topic sentences at the beginning or end of a paragraph, or inferred
- sequence of ideas within a paragraph
- carefully chosen words to clarify meanings (Bhuvaneswari, 2008, for a discussion on Psycho Linguistic Intervention Strategies).

Coursework in the pre-service English sequence need to be demanding. University students need to be highly proficient in possessing writing skills so that these may be adapted to the developmental level of the pupil as well as modeled later in the student teaching experience. Literature courses need to stress comprehension strategies and analyzing the study of novels in terms of characterization, setting, point of view, satire, and plot. Speaking experiences should reflect a clear voice with appropriate stress, pitch, juncture, and enunciation. In written work and in speaking activities, each undergraduate student must demonstrate proficiency and not fall through the cracks due to too many students being in a class. English professors need to be highly competent and take much interest in student achievement and progress. They need to meet periodically with each student to notice if proper standards and criteria are being achieved. The professor serves as a model for teaching and needs to show this model in diverse teaching situations (Ediger, 2007).

Prospective social studies teachers need to have a thorough grounding in the social sciences. Each of the following courses must be demanding and students must show that content is being mastered :

- history with its relevant past in the curriculum, in courses including World History, The Middle East, Latin American and American History, Asiatic as well as European History
- geography as a separate subject as well as being integrated into the history curriculum.
- economics with emphasis upon recessions, depressions, mortgage meltdowns, goods and services

- political science with studies of the role of government on the local, state, and national levels, as well as the United Nations
- anthropology/sociology with stress placed upon how culture affects the human being (Parker, 2001).

Each of the above social sciences has implications for human behaviour and how it influences the individual and group in society. Professors of the social sciences need to have high expectations for each student in possessing needed facts, concepts, and generalizations, useful for the self as a member in society and for teaching. They need to develop within students an understanding of salient knowledge and methods used to acquire content by social scientists.

Pre-service teachers must become proficient in content pertaining to the earth, physical, and biological sciences. They need to achieve excellence in course objectives in each of the above named sciences. Laboratory methods must be carefully supervised and a thorough process of evaluation of learner achievement and progress must be in evidence. Models of teaching quality by professors need to be there for pre-service teachers to emulate (Ediger, 2008a&b).

Mathematics in the general education sequence need to be taught indepth with careful monitoring by professors to assist in optimal student achievement and progress. It, again, is important to monitor carefully those who are planning to become teachers to reveal optimal attainment. Strong student effort and positive attitudes are always salient (Phillips, *et al.* 2008).

Undergraduate students need to engage in field experiences,directly related to the teaching of social studies in the public schools. Here, students may observe pupils in the classroom setting, work with small groups and individuals, evaluate the kinds of misunderstandings which pupils possess, and notice general progress made by learners. If the pre-service teacher will be teaching in a self-contained classroom, he/she should be involved in working with pupils in the different subject matter areas. Methods of teaching may and do cut across each academic discipline.

In the professional course sequence, pre-service teachers must experience educational psychology in its diverse manifestations. Undergraduate students should have ample opportunities to see how each of the following psychologies operates in actual teaching and learning situations :

- use of behaviorism and measurable stated objectives
- implementation of problem solving and project methods
- emphasis upon pupil choices and decision making in the curriculum as in learning centers
- holism in the instructional arena (Thiyagu, *et al.*, 2009).

A thorough grounding in the philosophy of education which stresses the following is also salient for prospective to teachers to not only study these schools of thought, but also see them operationalized :

- realism with emphasis placed upon measurably stated objectives in teaching
- existentialism stressing the human condition, as in literature
- idealism emphasizing the "categorical imperative" as viewed by Immanuel Kant
- experimentalism which integrates ideas in teaching pertaining to school and society (Dewey, 1916).

Educational psychology and philosophy courses become meaningful and challenging when practical applications are made of each in the public school classroom.

Measurement and evaluation course work needs to be meaningful and useful to pre-service teachers. Indepth learning and demonstrated accomplishment must be in the offing for the following, among others :

- writing and critiquing teacher written tests
- devising valid and reliable testing instruments to appraise pupil achievement in the social studies
- understanding the concepts of percentiles, standard deviation, the normal distribution curve, as well as quartile deviation
- attaching meaning to research studies involving experimental studies, correlations, and descriptive studies
- examining and appraising norm and criterion referenced tests
- evaluating the concepts formative and summative tests, as well as benchmarks of instruction (Ormrod, 2007).

Methods of teaching the social studies are highly significant and should be integrated with field experiences and seminars. Thus, pre-service teachers are assisted in applying what was learned in the university classroom. Methods of teaching the social studies should emphasize the following :

- unit construction based on sound research, educational psychology, and philosophical thought
- mini-lessons taught and appraised in the classroom setting
- field studies in which social studies methods are tried out in the public school classroom
- conferences held with the university supervisor pertaining to field work experiences in the social studies
- tests given to students to indicate achievement and progress in methods courses. Diagnosis and remediation is involved here (Reilly, 2007).

Professors teaching social studies methods courses need to present a model to prospective teachers who will be working with pupils in the public schools.

Student teaching is the capstone or final experience of the undergraduate sequence in education. Here, the student teacher needs to integrate and relate previous university experiences leading to :

- the pre-service teacher taking part in all responsibilities subsequently of a full time regular teacher.
- observing and participating in the classroom under the guidance of a quality cooperating teacher.
- managing a classroom of learners, grouping for instruction, and observing pupil achievement and progress.
- engaging pupils in meaningful learning.
- developing and designing units of study and daily lesson plans.
- assisting pupils in small groups and individual study.
- teaching in large group sessions.
- pupils self evaluation and responsible behaviour.
- interacting positively with the school administrator and with other classroom teachers (National Council for the Social Studies, 2008).

The student teacher needs to be appraised frequently by the university supervisor in order to improve instruction. Also, it is good to conduct a seminar with other student teachers supervised by the university supervisor during the semester. The seminar needs to include

- discussions on problems faced in student teaching and possible remedial actions taken
- suggestions for improving teaching and learning situations

- the use of teaching materials/experiences such as AV aids, DVDs, electronic readers, the internet, the world wide web, basal textbooks, excursions, among others.
- making of teaching aids to assist in the instructional arena.

Innovative methods of teaching to observe by the student teacher include :

- team teaching and flexible grouping.
- cooperative learning, as well as peer teaching and learning.
- problem solving, project methods, as well as critical and creative thinking situations.
- the integrated social studies curriculum.
- use of primary sources in teaching history (Pace, 2007).

Each of the above named plans need to be analyzed for discussion purposes. University students need to see the pros and cons of each plan.

IN CLOSING

The writer has drafted an outline of a proposal for developing a professional social studies teacher.

It cannot be emphasized too much that high quality is essential in these endeavors. Social studies teachers need to assist in developing knowledgeable good citizens who can function well in school and in society.

REFERENCES

Bhuvaneswari, S. (2008), Effect of Psycho Linguistic Intervention Strategies in Enhancing Writing Competency in English Among High school Learners. Alagappa University, Karaikudi, India. Ph D thesis appraised by the writer.

Dewey, John (1916), *Democracy and Education*. New York: The Macmillan Company.

Ediger, Marlow (2007), *Language Arts Education*. New Delhi, India: Discovery Publishing House.

Ediger, Marlow (2008a), "Leadership in the School Setting," Education, 129 (1), 17-20.

Ediger, Marlow (2008b), "The Old Order Amish and the Social Studies," *Viewpoints*, 38 (4), 14-16.

National Council for the Social Studies (2008), "A Vision of Powerful Teaching and Learning in the Social Studies," *Social Education*, 72 (5), 277-280.

Ormrod, Jeanne Ellis (2007), *Educational Psychology*, Sixth Edition, Chapter Twelve.

Pace, Judith L. (December 18, S2007), "Why We Need To Save (and Strengthen), Social Studies," *Education Week*.

Parker, Walter C. (2001), *Social Studies in Elementary Education*. Upper Saddle River, New Jersey: Charles E. Merrill.

Phillips, et. al. (2008), "Enhancing a Curriculum: A Focus on the Developmental Process," *College Student Journal*, 42(4), 1070-1074.

Reilly, Mary Ann (2007), "Choice of Action: Using Data to Make Instructional decisions in Kindergarten," *The Reading Teacher*, 60 (8), 770-775.

Thyagu *et al.* (2009), "Mobile Learning is Future Learning," Edutracks, 8 (6), 5-8.

Parent/Teacher Conferences in Social Studies 14

Quality communication is needed between the parents and the school. Lines of communication need to be kept open. To often, there are hindrances to open communication due to time factors, inconsiderateness, rudeness, and haste. If pupils are to do well in school, there needs to be feelings that parentAeacher conferences are important. Too frequently, social studies is minimized or eliminated from communication time with parents. Traditional beliefs remain that the three r's (reading, writing, and arithmetic) are the only basics in the curriculum, but that indeed has narrowed the scope of the curriculum. Social studies has as a major objective to develop good citizenship which is so necessary in the global world. Accurate communication is important here, as well as in parent/teacher conference (Ediger, 2002).

Communicating Effectively

Which ingredients make for having ideas move freely from a sender to a receiver? Certainly, there are impediments to quality communication. These need to be removed or minimized as much as possible. Pleasant manners with an accompanying speaking voice which indicates consideration for others is salient. The manners incorporate non-verbal communication and need to be analyzed. Do they attract or repel others? Nervous gestures and facial expressions might well hinder effective communication. Teachers in a school need to see models of effective non-verbal as well as those which are ineffective on video-tape. Committees of teachers then need to discuss the "why" for each. Studying exemplars of quality parent/teacher conferences from appropriate reference sources in educational journals and teacher education textbooks provide guidelines for the ongoing discussion (Ediger, 2009).

It might be worth the expenditure to have consultant come in to assist with inservice education in conducting parent/ teacher conferences. Roles may be played of the teacher and of the parent in the simulated environment. Problem areas are then identified and solutions sought. Involved problems include what kinds of information the teacher wishes to convey to parents such as pupil information on economic concepts within an ongoing unit of study :

- goods, services, mortgages, liens, foreclosures, indebtedness,
- credit cards, interest, toxic loans, lender, borrower
- payments, ATM machines, finance managing.

Sharing of ideas needs much stress during a parent/ teacher conference. The concerns of parents require careful listening by the teacher in order that these may addressed. Perhaps, the parent is concerned about the lack of friends of the involved child. A framework might well be agreed upon to assist in friendship building. The child needs to be placed into a small group which is highly accepting of others in a social studies unit. A major concern of the teacher might emphasize that the child become a better listener. With the home and the school working together, solutions must be found to address problems identified during a parent/teacher conference. Then too, problems may be addressed at any time during the school year through :

- *e-mail.* The e-mail may be sent during a teacher's convenient time. Communication may occur as frequently as desired.
- *telephone calls, either land line or cellular.* The call may even deal with congratulating a child for doing well on a social studies project. Voice recorders are handy when either the parent or the teacher cannot come to the phone at the time of calling.
- *faxing messages* in terms of necessary communication items, between home and school too, is becoming increasingly common.

There are numerous formal opportunities for parents to come to school and visit with involved teachers. These include :

- open house whereby samples of pupil work in the social studies may be displayed for the parent to view
- parent/teacher organizations in which the former has an opportunity to visit with the social studies teacher (Parker, 2001).

Quality communication between home and school is necessary in order to work together to provide the best learnings possible in the social studies. The objectives, learning activities to achieve the chosen ends, and the evaluation procedures, need to be clarified and made meaningful to parents. The latter has an inward desire, generally, to assist their offspring to attain optimally. There is much the home can do to foster better achievement among offspring. At a very young age, the parent needs to read orally to the child using appropriate enunciation. Reading aloud with proper stress, pitch, and juncture provides a model to the young child in learning to love social studies library books. The duration of the read aloud should not exceed the intrinsic interests of the young learner. The latter will have a short, attention span which needs to be adhered to. With older pupils, the parent and the learner need to engage in reciprocal reading whereby each reads a portion of the library book in sequence. Questions raised need to be discussed and meaning established. Pupils learn much social studies content by reading carefully selected library books. The library books should deal with a variety of genera and appropriate reading levels of the involved pupil (Kennedy, 2006).

Within the framework of parent/teacher conferences, much emphasis needs to be placed upon what both the home and the school can do to aid pupil progress. A follow through of the conference allows for evaluation in terms of its effectiveness. Additional ways the home and school can work together are the following :

- set up a plan, cooperatively, to assist pupils, for example, to improve in oral communication. Specific goals must be set with accompanying learning opportunities.
- determine ways to motivate pupil learning in the home setting, such as rewarding pupils for "x" number of library books read.
- take pupils on short excursions in the neighborhood to see salient sites, such as a museum. Discuss with pupils observations made.
- assist pupils to write up observations made, such as the excursion taken which is named above.
- make models of what has been read/studied in the home setting, such as a model parthenon pertaining to learnings on Greece.
- do a booklet on learning opportunities, experienced in the home setting. This provides excellent activities in using the internet and the word processor (See Dykstra, 2008).

The Portfolio in Communicating Achievement

A portfolio may be an excellent approach in evaluating pupil achievement in the social studies. Doing an electronic portfolio adds to the interests of doing things in the social studies. A portfolio developed by pupils with teacher assistance houses salient documents of pupil learning and progress. Thus, representative entries such as the following may be made in a social studies portfolio :

- summaries of book reports and other written work.
- outlines developed of salient subject matter.
- test results from teacher prepared tests.
- electronic photos of completed art work as well as construction projects, and photo essays.
- recordings of reader's theater, oral reading, and of creative dramatizations.

From the above, there are excellent possibilities for informal as well as formal parent/teacher conferences. In number one asterisk above, for example, parents may look at the quality of written work and progress made from one paper to the next. Significant facets to view in the evaluation process might well include the following :

- sequence of ideas expressed in written work.
- quality of spelling of words, including the use of spell checkers.
- agreement of subject and predicate.
- correct placement of modifiers.
- proper use of punctuation marks.

What is evaluated will depend, too, upon the developmental level of tht pupil. There need to be high, but not unreasonable expectations for each pupil. Challenging goals need to be achievable. Based on the portfolio results, the parent and the social studies teacher need to agree upon several goals for the pupil to attain. At a subsequent conference, it can be noticed if these gaps have been eliminated (Ediger, 2007).

Report Cards to Report Pupil Progress

The traditional report card, issued every six weeks approximately, has some merits in its use. Together with other methods used to report pupil achievement, it might still be operational. The categories on the report card to convey pupil information on achievement may need to be modified. There are a plethora of questions which a parent may have as a result of viewing the report card, indicating six weeks in duration. Which are salient categories for reporting progress in the social studies? The following are a few which the writer has noticed on pupil report cards pertaining to all curriculum areas :

- puts for much effort in learning.
- perseveres in whatever is being studied.
- solves personal problems.
- gets along well with others.
- works well with pupils in a committee setting (Crawford, 2008).

Then there are other categories of evaluation pertaining to the social studies only, such as :

- reads library books and other social studies materials during spare time
- likes social studies as a curriculum area
- tends to work to his/her capacity in social studies achievement
- volunteers to do extra work in ongoing lessons
- writes on the social studies when a writing topic may be chosen
- understands significant concepts in the social studies
- develops a well made project for the annual social studies fair (a note might be attached to the report card pertaining to this yearly item).

Pertaining to the first asterisked item above, for example, a rating needs to be given on a five point scale. By looking at the ratings, the parent receives some idea as to how well the offspring is doing in each category. Areas of weakness need to be discussed with the parent and needed modifications made. If, for example, the child is weak in "likes social studies as a curriculum area", both the parent and the teacher need to brainstorm as to what might be done to change pupil behaviour in this case (Ryan, 2006).

REFERENCES

Crawford, Marilyn (2008), "Think Inside the Clock," *Phi Delta Kappan*, 90(4), 251-255.

Dykstra, Dee Vee E. (2008), "Integrating Critical Thinking and Memorandum Writing Into Course Curriculum Using the Internet as a Research Tool," *College Student Journal*, 42 (3), 920-929.

Ediger, Marlow (2002), *Teaching Social Studies Successfully*. New Delhi, India: Discovery Publishing House.

Ediger, Marlow (2007), "Meaning in Reading Instruction," *Reading Improvement*, 44 (4), 217-220.

Ediger, Marlow (2009), "Scope in the Social Studies," Edutracks, 8.

Kennedy, Mary (2007), "From Teacher Quality to Teaching Quality," *Educational Leadership*, 63 (6), 14-19.

Parker, Walter (2001), *Social Studies in Elementary Education*. Upper Saddle River, New Jersey: The MacMillan Company.

Ryan, Tracey E. (2006), "Motivating Novice Students to Read Their Textbooks," *Journal of Instructional Psychology*, 33(1), 135-140.

Reading Comprehension in Social Studies

15

Being able to read well is vital in the social studies. It is a valuable way of learning from the social sciences which provide content for the social studies curriculum. Pupils then need to become proficient in reading. Reading consists of word recognition as well as comprehension of ideas. Both must be stressed adequately in assisting the pupil to become a good reader in the social studies. This does not mean that the social studies becomes a reading course, but rather it facilitates the learning process in achieving relevant ideas. Subject matter learnings should facilitate the pupil becoming a knowledgeable, good citizen in society. Quality attitudes, too, are then acquired when pupils achieve relevant objectives of instruction Ediger, 2002).

Readiness for Reading

An important consideration in assisting pupils to read social studies content is that needed prerequisites have been emphasized. Thus, pupils need to possess adequate background information. Building background information within pupils prior reading in an ensuing lesson helps the pupil to relate the new with what was previously learned. This also guides pupils to relate the new content to the self.

Thus, the ensuing lesson must make sense to the involved learner. Background information may be provided by looking at illustrations on the same page as the scripted ideas to be read in the basal social studies textbook. Additional experiences in providing background information pertains to using a related video-tape which clarifies subject matter content (National Council for Geographic Education, 1994).

Readiness activities also stress pupils seeing the new words in print, prior to reading. These may be printed on the white board, use of the overhead projector, or on a screen with the enlarged words, through computer use. Pupils may then practice saying the printed words aloud, as well as using them in sentences.

A last readiness item is for pupils to identify questions they would like answered from the reading experience. Answers may be discussed as a followup. Indepth discussions might well lead to using a variety of reference sources to secure additional information. -Branching out and extending learnings is to be welcomed, especially with involved pupil interests (Roy, 2009).

Word Recognition in the Social Studies

Which word recognition techniques are salient for pupils to master? This depends upon the needs of pupils and which might also mean that there are common word recognition needs for all to attain. Word recognition should be taught in context, if at all possible. Problems in word recognition are then fresh in the minds of learners. If a pupil in a unit titled "The Middle Ages" is not identifying the word "guild in print," his/her attention should be drawn to the beginning letter "g" to notice its related sound which may either be the soft or hard "g" sound. Sometimes, the basal provides a phonetic spelling for the possible unknown word like "gild," not the soft "g" sound as in "jild." It may become necessary to immediately pronounce the correct word to a pupil so he/she does not lose meaning in ideas read. For a word such as "manor," the letter "m" has a highly consistent sound. Here, a pupil may benefit much from using phonics with the consistency between symbol and sound. There are familiar words which begin with the "m" sound and are familiar to lerners.. Then too, the word 'manor[1] has a shorter word contained therein as in "man." There are a plethora of words ending in "or" with which pupils are familiar such as "tailor" and "favor." The pupil might then put together "man" and the "or" ending to make "manor." Both words (guild and manor), along with others, may be placed on a word wall in the classroom for future reference (Ediger, 2007).

Use of context clues are the best means for a reader to use in identifying the unknown. Thus, the pupil may be reading, "The (unknown word) lived on a manor." If the pupil notices the letter "s" and tries diverse words which fit in with the rest of the words in the sentence and paragraph, the chances are he/she will come up with the word "serf." Then too, "serf" is spelled quite consisntly phonetically. The "er" sound is familiar in many words such as baker, barber. Noblemen, slaves, serfs, knights, and journeyman are words associated with the Middle Ages. These words may be added to the word wall as they are met in print by the learner. Pupils need to relate their lives in society with present day farmers being related in duties in life on a manor, knighthood to soldiering and the military, and guilds to manufacturing of products such as shoes, blankets, silver trays, dishes, among others. Guild members also provided services such as being a barber or meat cutter (Reilly, 2008).

If pupils are struggling readers in the social studies, the basal text print may be enlarged by an opaque projector, with selected content reflected on a large screen. All pupils being taught, here, in a small group need to see the words clearly and pay careful attention as the teacher reads the content aloud as he/she points to each word. This may be repeated with pupils joining the read aloud.Thus, pupils may read the ensuing ideas without stumbling on individual words and thus lose interest in the subject-matter. The writer when supervising university student teachers has noticed the following in pupils reading from the basal as supervised by the student teacher and the cooperating teacher :

- teachers reading aloud salient passages to a few struggling readers as the latter follow along in the basal textbook.
- pupils following along in their textbooks as an accompanying DVD plays the scripted ideas. Electronic aids are making the act of reading more suitable to the individual's present reading level.
- teachers scaffolding print for children. Thus with scaffolding, a pupil may understand more complex ideas as compared to what is printed. Intervening ideas may be presented to bridge subject matter extending that which exists in print, compared to an ideal envisioned by the teacher in teaching the social studies.
- a good reader reading aloud selected content to others who need assistance. Those receiving the assistance need to look at each word carefully as it is being read.

To promote interest in reading, the teacher needs to display relevant social studies library books, and talk briefly about a few books to whet pupil attitudes for reading. Pupils individually then choose their very own library books to read. These might be read during the pupil's spare time or be taken home for reading, if read during a pupil's spare time, the social studies teacher may ask the learner a few relevant questions covering the content to notice comprehension as well as interest in reading. There are teachers who devote fifteen to thirty minutes a day in sustained silent reading (SSR). During this time, children may learn much social studies content on history, geography, sociology/anthropology, economics, and political science. As a pupil in grade and high school, the writer enjoyed free time fir choosing self selected reading materials. If the pupil can choose social studies library books to read during spare time in school as well as in the home setting, reading skills, and knowledge about the social studies should increase dramatically (See Cellano and Neuman).

Parent-Teacher Conferences

Parent/teacher conferences should include how well a learner is doing in knowledge, skills, and attitudinal acquisition. Growth in knowledge objectives in the social studies should include the following :

- how well a child is achieving major facts, concepts and generalizations in ongoing units of study?
- how much time is devoted to reading library books pertaining to the social studies?
- how much effort is put forth in understanding main ideas?

The above-named asterisked items may be subdivided such as in concepts developed. In any unit of study, there are vital concepts to attach meaning to, as in the Middle Ages. Thus concepts such as the following may bridge the gap between the past and the present :

- methods of farming used
- occupations, then and now
- means of transportation, contrasting the Middle Ages with the present.

Skills objectives may be broken down into categories of demonstrated improvement in sequence, as well as that which needs further emphasis. Then too, specific learner needs in reading social studies subject matter may be analyzed into component parts with evaluation of pupil achievement each facet being important. Thus, the following may be analyzed in terms of pupil progress :

- use of context clues to identify unknown words
- looks for smaller words within a longer word to identify the unknown
- develops skills in phonic use to recognize the unknown word
- understands what is being read
- is able to summarize orally or in writing what has been read silently.

Attitudinal objectives which are salient to achieve include the following :

- reads social studies library books for enjoyment
- has good attitudes toward reading from the basal
- wants to identify unknown words
- has an inward desire to read increasingly complex ideas (Ediger, 2008).

IN CLOSING

Reading is a very important way of learning in the social studies. Other methods, too, need to be stressed in ongoing units of study such as the following :

- power point presentations and video-tapes related to ongoing units of study
- DVDs, CDs, podcasts, and internet sources
- knowledgeable resource personnel.

Thus, a multi-media approach should assist pupils to achieve more optimally.

REFERENCES

Cellano, Donna, and Susan B. Neuman (2008), "When Schools Close, the Knowledge Gap Grows," *Phi Delta Kappan*, 94 (4), 256-262.

Ediger, Marlow (2002), *Teaching Social Studies Successfully*. New Delhi, India: Discovery Publishing House.

Ediger, Marlow (2007),"Meaning in Reading Instruction," *Reading Improvement*, 44 (4), 217-220.

Ediger, Marlow (2008), "Leadership in the School Setting," *Education*, 129(1), 17-20.

National Council for Geographic Education (1994), *Geography for Life*. Washington, DC: NCGE.

Reilly, Mary Ann (2008), "Teaching the Right Words : Art Conversations and Poetry," *Language Arts*, 86 (2), 99-107).

Roy, Ruma (2009), "New Challenges in Teacher Education" *Edutracks*, 8 (6), 19-20.

Sequence in Social Studies 16

Quality sequence in the social studies is of utmost importance. Sequence emphasizes "when" selected concepts should be stressed in ongoing lessons and units of study. The social studies teacher needs to observe pupils carefully in teaching and learning situations to ascertain suitable, ordered experiences for pupils. Pupils face frustration if the learning opportunities are too complex and may feel boredom if the tasks are too easy. Carefully sequenced facts, concepts, and generalizations assist pupils to attain more optimally, be it in programmed learning or in open ended approaches. What might the social studies teacher do to assist pupils achieve more optimally in the social studies?

Diverse Plans in Determining Sequence in the Social Studies

Programmed learning stresses that the programmer determines objectives, learning activities, and evaluation procedures, in a particular order. The learning activities are very closely aligned with the objectives and move from the simple to the complex in a tightly planned sequence. Pupils make few mistakes in a pilot studied, published programme.

Thus, for example, a pupil at a computer terminal, reads a few sentences, then responds to a multiple choice test item, covering what has been read. He/she immediately receives an answer of being either correct/incorrect. If incorrect, the pupil sees the correct answer on the monitor and is also ready for the next sequential learning. This sequence of read, respond, and check is followed continuously. Each learning builds on the previously sequential subject matter content acquired by pupils. By carefully sequencing information from one step of learning to the next, the pupil experiences much sequential success. The emphasis here is upon responding correctly, which reinforces each step of learning. Operant conditioning is then in evidence. The late B. F. Skinner was a leading exponent of programmed learning and operant conditioning (Ediger, 2003).

Teaching toward mandated objectives is more open ended as compared to operant conditioning, but it still stresses the teacher focusing upon closure in terms of pupils achieving what is measurable. Pupils, here, take annual tests containing multiple choice test items. The test items are aligned with precise or specific objectives of instruction. This has made it that teachers attempt to teach toward the specific objectives only, so that pupils score higher on the mandated, required tests. The scope of the curriculum is delimited to that which is tested. Sequence in teaching then pertains to the order of objectives pupils are to attain. Measurable test results are emphasized in the use of programmed learning as well as in the mandated objectives curriculum (Ediger, 2007).

Toward the other end of the continuum are problem solving methods, quite popular today, in teaching the social studies. Problem solving is rather open ended in that within an ongoing lesson/unit of study, pupils choose a problem to solve. The problem is salient and requires effort and deliberation in its solving. A variety of references are used to gather necessary information. They include the internet, basal social studies textbooks, encyclopedia entries, library books, and knowledgeable personnel, among others. The information is organized to be used in securing an answer to the problem. The answer, here, becomes a tentative hypothesis to be tested. If the tentative answer holds up under scrutiny due to critical and creative thinking, then it is accepted. If not, the original hypothesis is modified or refuted. Problem solving is flexible, and is sequenced by learners with teacher guidance. John Dewey (1859-1953) was a leading advocate of problem solving (Dewey, 1916).

The project method is closely related to problem-solving approaches and stresses that pupils, also, largely sequence their own work in ongoing social studies units of study. Here, within an ongoing unit of study, pupils choose a project to develop with teacher assistance. The project generally stresses a small group endeavor which tends to emphasize a construction activity. The activity has relevance to the involved learners and possesses a perceived purpose to these pupils. The project then is not emphasized for the sake of doing so, but rather to fulfil a need. Carefully planning is necessary and stresses cooperation among pupils. The plans are carried out with modifications as needed. The final product is then appraised in terms of desired criteria. A project activity approach in learning is highly pupil centered with sequence residing within the learner as he/she works within the group to plan, develop, and evaluate the purposeful project (Sharma and Sharma, 2009).

Constructivism in teaching the social studies emphasizes that pupils create their own knowledge as a lesson or unit progresses. With enriched experiences, the pupil gains knowledge to develop more comprehensive concepts and generalizations. There are no absolutes, the pupil continues to achieve, grow, and develop in a stimulating social studies environment. The teacher is a guide and helper of pupil progress, not one who lectures or has precise predetermined objectives stated prior to teaching for learner attainment. With constructivism, learning is ongoing and cannot be measured, but through teacher observation assistance is given as needed to motivate and encourage learning. Motivation comes from within the pupil as he/she sequences achievement in the social studies (Parker, 2001).

Problem solving, project methods, and constructivism do not emphasize measurable results from pupil learning. Objectives, here, are not predetermined and stressed prior to teaching and learning situations. The doing part is sequenced by the learner with teacher guidance.

Basal textbook methodology comes between behaviorism (programmed learning/mandated objectives philosophy of instruction) and action centered curricula (problem-solving, project methods, and constructivism). A well and carefully chosen basal social studies textbook may be used as presented in the accompanying manual or modified to meet personal needs of pupils. Thus, the manual contains objectives for pupil attainment, learning opportunities to achieve the objectives, as well as evaluation procedures to provide feedback to teachers on pupil progress. Generally, social studies teachers feel the subject matter contained in each unit of study in the textbook needs extension and elaboration. The subject matter may come from the internet, reputable encyclopedias, library books, excursions, informed persons, and AV aids, among other sources (Association for Supervision and Curriculum Development, 2007). The basal textbook then :

- contains a structure with related ideas in designing and teaching the ongoing social studies unit
- provides opportunities to clarify and amplify subject matter content
- emphasizes a revised sequence to aid more optimal learner achievement.

Students should be challenged to raise questions pertaining to subject matter studied from the basal. These questions may well lead to searching for indepth information leading to critical and creative thinking.

When reading subject matter from the basal, the teacher needs to provide assistance in word recognition and comprehension of ideas. The following word recognition techniques should be stressed as needed :

- context clues to identify unknown words?
- phonics to use as clues to unlock new words?
- syllabication skills such as noticing root words, prefixes and suffixes and thus identify the unknown word?
- noticing short words within the larger word to aid and identify the unfamiliar (Baumann, *et al.*, 2007).

Subject matter needs to be read with appropriate stress, pitch, and enunciation to avoid monotony and read with enthusiasm! Social studies can be an enjoyable academic area to study when :

- the content is related to the personal lives of pupils
- pupils relate content studied to other people, nations, regions, and continents in the world.

The above named relationships aid pupils in attaining quality sequence, especially when relating it to their own personal lives. This makes the study of the social studies meaningful indeed! The personal talents and abilities, too, may be brought into each social studies unit as it enriches sequential learnings. The following talents, as examples, might well then be integrated :

- artistic to show scenes and situations being studied, such as well known persons in history, using a variety of art media.
- verbal as in reading and reporting on library books such studying people of other cultures.
- analytical, synthesis, objective, and logical thinking skills in organizing and forming ideas.

- collaborative skills in working with other learners in an ongoing activity.
- manual dexterity to show abilities within concrete experiences.
- technology skills to gather subject matter from a variety of electronic sources.
- mathematical talents in measuring and doing construction work related directly to an ongoing unit of study (Gardner, 1993).

CONCLUSION

Social studies teachers need to study learners in diverse kinds of situations to ascertain the best way to emphasize quality sequence in learning. Sequence stresses "when" is the optimal time to engage pupils in ensuing learnings. New learnings should not be too complex, nor too easy, but at a level which is challenging and yet the ensuing objectives are achievable.

REFERENCES

Association for Supervision and Curriculum Development (2007), *Education Update*, 49 (3), 1, 8.

Baugmann, James R, *et al.* (2007), "Bumping Into Spicy, Tasty Words That Catch Your Tongue: A Formative Experiment on Vocabulary Instruction," *The Reading Teacher*, 61 (2), 108-124.

Dewey, John (1916) *Democracy and Education*. New York: Macmillan Publishing Company.

Ediger, Marlow (2002) *Teaching Social Studies Successfully*. New Delhi, India: Discovery Publishing House.

Ediger, Marlow (2003), *Psychology and Curriculum*. New Delhi, India: Discovery Publishing House.

Ediger, Marlow (2007), "Learning Activities in the Curriculum," *College Student Journal*, 41 (4), 967-969.

Gardner, Howard (1993), *Multiple Intelligences: Theory Into Practice.* New York: Basic Books.

Parker, Walter C. (2001), *Social Studies in Elementary Education.* Upper Saddle River, New Jersey: Prentice Hall, Inc.

Sharma, Mala, and Suman Sharma (2009), "Attitude of Science Teachers Toward the Project Method," *Edutracks*, 8 (6), 40-43.

Metacognition Strategies in Social Studies

17

Teachers are always looking for approaches to use in assisting students to remember and integrate leanings more effectively of what has been learned previously. Meaningful learnings accrue when students perceive knowledge as being related, rather than in isolation. The social studies teacher has important responsibilities in assisting students to understand facts, concepts, and generalizations in ongoing lessons and units of study. Metacognition strategies then need to be in the offing.

Metacognition Strategies

Students need to be able to think about thinking. Thus, the student is aided to reflect upon previous learnings experienced. This involves thought and thinking. Metacognition is needed for student achievement, growth, and progress in school and in society. Learners then acquire what is practical and useful. Inert ideas are not salient and become useless (Savithiri, 2006).

Social studies has its roots in society and provides human made knowledge, skills, and attitudes for life and living. What is practical can be expressed in abstract thought such as ideas in history, geography, political science, economics as well as in anthropology/sociology. Each of these academic disciplines contains structural ideas which provide a basis for further divisions and sub-divisions and assists in understanding human behaviour more thoroughly. Thus, the following summary statements from each social science discipline listed above provide the student with ideas for thinking indepth :

- history - a study of selected, relevant events of the past, using primary and secondary sources
- geography - a study of regions on the planet earth and how humans interact with the natural environment
- political science - a study of how rules, regulations, and law affect and impact people at different levels of government
- economics - a study of the production, distribution, and consumption of goods and services
- anthropology/sociology - a study of how the human made environment (culture) affects groups and individuals (Parker, 2001).

Social studies lessons and units of study need to incorporate these ideas in scope and sequence, as well as provide opportunities for reflection. Reflection involves metacognition, to think about thinking. Whatever the student has acquired and learned, adequate time must be given to think and view anew and in a creative manner about that which is vital. In studying the Ottoman Empire, its collapse and aftermath in 1918, as an example pertaining to history, the student needs assistance to reflect upon the following key ideas :

- how problems arose in terms of its divisions among superpowers in that France received a Mandate from the League of Nations to rule Lebanon and Syria
- Great Britain received a Mandate to rule the land of Palestine, Trans-Jordan, and Iraq
- The Balfour Declaration was passed which provided a homeland for the Jews in the land of Palestine

- The Arabs in Palestine opposed the Balfour Declaration since they had a population of 640,000 inhabitants while the Jews numbered 80,000 in Palestine.
- With an influx of migrating Jews to Palestine, the Arabs felt threatened.
- Adolph Hitler became Chancellor of Germany in 1933. His anti-Semetic policies toward Jews forced many to leave Germany, with many going to Palestine.
- The Arabs saw many Jews coming to Palestine and changing the ratio of Arabs to Jews. Tensions started to rise between the two nationalities.
- The outbreak of World War II in 1939 brought some relief to the tension; Great Britain and France were at war with Nazi Germany. The Jews felt loyalty to Great Britain whereas the Arabs had feelings of neutrality toward Great Britain due to the latter's agreement to the Balfour Declaration (Palestine Royal Commission, 1937).

Metacognition's emphasis upon one's own mental processes stresses the student throughly concentrating upon the above and related major ideas in a social studies unit on The Middle East. It involves a learner centred curriculum. The learner reflects upon cognitive learnings, pondering over such ideas as, "How and why did France and Great Britain receive mandates from the League of Nations?" By reflecting upon the "how" and "why," the learner does indepth thinking and also extends vocabulary understandings. The concepts of "mandate" and "League of Nations" also involve cognition. The student thinks about thinking and what was learned about these concepts and raises questions such as, "Were Syria, Lebanon, Palestine, and Trans-Jordan not able or ready to govern themselves after the conclusion of World War One, without foreign rule?" A new synthesis is developed between previous learnings acquired and the ensuing ideas gained through metacognition. Or as another question, why the Arabs felt threatened with the increasing number of Jews coming to Palestine. This might well have included doing internet research on this topic. When reading related ideas, the student monitors his/her own progress by noticing if the subject matter is being comprehended. The learner then rehearses what was read to notice comprehension. A student centered approach is inherent in that he/she depends upon the self to monitor comprehension just as the learner rethinks what was learned and creatively comes up with questions requiring new knowledge in the cognitive domain. With metacognition, the student thinks about what was achieved in terms of previously acquired facts, concepts, and generalizations. This promotes integration of content when new ideas are forthcoming. The student develops feelings of self efficacy or feelings of confidence in the self to achieve and learn effectively (Bandura, 1997).

Problem-solving, too, may be emphasized as a result of metacognition. From the asterisked items above, the rise of Adolph Hitler in Germany might well provide information for problem solving activities. For example, a student individually or students collectively may identify the problem," Why did Adolph Hitler gain power in Germany and how did his rule affect the Jewish people?" Learners might then develop an hypothesis which may be tested by securing information from a variety of reference sources. The committee may accept or revise the hypothesis. In the long run, hypotheses are tentative and subject to change, but for the present time, students do obtain answers to their identified problems. Problem solving indicates that there are no absolutes, but finding information is continuous in the search for truths (Dewey, 1916).

Growth and development are ongoing in any human being. The individual modifies his/her thinking through reflection. New ideas are then being developed. Monitoring one's thinking pertains to noticing if one is comprehending and securing information in the cognitive domain. Metacognition emphasizes reflecting upon what was achieved. This assists the student to attain creative understanding of facts, concepts, and generalizations. Memory of previous learnings achieved aids when reflection occurs.

Perception is involved when the learner experiences sounds, feelings, appearances and objects, among others. These perceptions provide a basis for actions, meditation, and learning. Meaningful experiences then may accrue in the curriculum. Project methods might be used to facilitate perceptions. A doing approach is involved here. A need exists to fulfill a gap in learning. Students then perceive a purpose to construct, dramatize, and/or make something in an ongoing unit of study. These items then need careful planning to encourage quality work. The plans are fulfilled with the actual implementation of the perceived purpose. Evaluation in terms of quality criteria stresses if objectives have been met in doing the project. These criteria might well include the following :

- maximum effort put forth in doing the project.
- each one participating optimally in project development
- neatness in work quality.
- students working together harmoniously (Ediger, 2008).

Respect for others is of utmost importance. Rudeness, abrupt behaviour, lack of caring for others, and harassment need to be outlawed. During the time, the project is being pursued as well as completed, metacognition is being emphasized. The student thinks about how the processes were ongoing and makes revisions as needed. Thus, the learner assesses :

- how the project was decided upon?
- how the involved steps were sequenced?
- what conclusions were realized?
- which major concepts and generalizations were attained? (Ediger, 2005)

With metacognition strategies, the student monitors his/her ongoing achievement. If the student does not progress continuously in a given activity, the involved learner is aware of this occurring. The lack of concentrating and comprehending is a conscious factor. With careful monitoring, the student modifies and makes changes to facilitate more optimal progress. The student does this by reflecting upon previous experiences. It is highly worthwhile for the teacher to stress metacognition strategies in the curriculum.

REFERENCES

Bandura, Albert (1997), *Self-Efficacy The Exercise of Control*. New York: W. H. Freeman and Company.

Dewey, John (1916), *Democracy and Education*. New York: The Macmillan Company.

Ediger, Marlow (2005), "Themes to Emphasize in the Geography Curriculum," *Journal of Instructional Psychology*, 32 (2), 160-163.

Ediger, Marlow (2008), "Mental Health in the Curriculum," *Journal of Instructional Psychology*, 35 (1), 38- 42.

Palestine Royal Commission Report (1937). His Majesty's Stationery Office, London England, 404 pp. Received as a gift while serving as a teacher at Friend's Boys School, Ramallah, Jordan, 1953-1954.

Parker, Walter C. (2001), *Social Studies in Elementary Education*. Upper Saddle River, New Jersey: Prentice Hall, Inc.

Savithiri, V. (2006), Impact of Metacognitive Strategies in Enhancing Perceptual Skills Among High School Students on Learning Geometry, Ph D thesis evaluated by the writer for Alagappa University, Karaikudi, India.

Meaning in Social Studies 18

An important factor in teaching social studies is to develop meaningful learnings for pupils. Thus, pupils must understand what is taught. Through a variety of developmentally appropriate activities, pupils may attach meaning to relevant facts, concepts, and generalizations, as well as skills. They should help pupils to attain vital objectives of instruction. With valid and reliable means of evaluation, social studies teachers may ascertain if pupils have been successful achievers. Quality principles of learning must be used in teaching to guide more optimal pupil achievement and progress.

Meaning, the Pupil, and the Social Studies

When assisting pupils in reading social studies subject matter, teacher first must assist pupils to possess adequate background knowledge. The background knowledge relates directly to the ensuing content to be read. Relating the new content to that previously acquired, helps pupils to perceive the relationship of knowledge. Meaningful learnings then accrue. By looking at the illustrations in the basal, pupils may be motivated to predict what will be in the new content. These predictions may be checked with subject matter acquired after the content has been read (Ediger and Rao, 2000).

In addition to providing background information for reading the ensuing subject-matter, the teacher also needs to assist pupils with recognizing new words to be met in print. The new words may be printed on the chalkboard or via computer and magnified on the screen. Each of these words needs to be used in sentences as they appear in the basal. Thus, familiarity with word identification will enable a pupil to recognize each new word as the ensuing reading activity progresses.

As a follow-up experience, pupils with teacher guidance may use the subject matter read in :

- developing an experience chart, summarizing major conclusions from a discussion.
- making models from paper mache[1] or molding, moist paper towels.
- doing a continuing classroom book on content learned from sequential social studies units of study.
- taking a teacher and/or pupil made test to evaluate comprehension.
- placing new words on a classroom word wall (Ediger, 2008).

Technology might well take an equally important role as do traditional methods of having pupils read subject matter. This may especially be helpful to pupils with reading difficulties. Thus, electronic texts need to be in the offing in the social studies. With computer and software use, pupils may experience the following :

- the subject-matter read aloud while pupils follow along with the printed script on the monitor.
- music and animation to go along with the contents.
- new words pronounced. Words and definitions, or within contextual sentences, may be provided by the computer with a click of the mouse.

- computer technology can do away with problems of word recognition and the necessity to wait for assistance from a busy social studies teacher.
- tests from the computer may assess learner progress. Test results are stored by the computer to notice specific kinds of pupil errors for diagnostic purposes and for learner progress in achievement (Rhodes and Milby, 2007).

When readiness is in evidence, pupils may also be guided to achieve higher levels of cognition. This includes critical thinking in separating facts from opinions, fantasy from reality, and accurate from inaccurate information. Creative thinking, too, might well be emphasized. Here, pupils are challenged to come up with new, unique ideas. Novel ideas are needed in society which can make for innovations in school and in society. Critical and creative thinking are necessary to solve environmental problems, offer solutions to settle disputes between and among individuals and nations, as well as to use resources wisely. The following problems, also, need solutions within a state or nation :

- what to do about the national debt,
- solving the housing/mortgage crises,
- how to tax people equitably,
- emphasis upon more full employment,
- solving disagreements within and outside a nation through diplomatic channels,
- saving the environment and natural resources, including much attention paid to global warming (National Council for the Social Studies, 1994).

The above are key problems in the natural and social world. Lessons and units might well be built around these identified problem areas. A good current events program should aid pupils in making intelligent decisions. Knowledge objectives are important, but so are skills ends including analytic, synthetic, and evaluative objectives. Facts, alone are not adequate, but higher levels of cognition are needed in a quality current events program. Meaningful learnings are salient. Traditional methods as well as computerized approaches may be used in guiding pupils to higher cognitive levels of thought.

Monitoring, Reflecting, and Metacognition

When pupils read or participate in other learning activities, they should learn to monitor their own individual progress. Here, the pupil, when reading for example, will continually notice if comprehension is taking place and not word calling only. When reading is done, the reader wants to understand that which is read. Too frequently, a pupil is reading social studies subject matter, but fails to attach meaning to ideas being read. The same may be said about participating in discussions, the pupil must understand its contents or time is being wasted. By monitoring, the pupil assesses ongoing comprehension. Then too, the pupil needs to reflect upon content read or discussed. When reflection is taking place, the pupil rehearses and analyzes subject matter from content read or discussed. Review is taking place and this helps the learner to retain ideas. Use is made of previously acquired subject matter.

Metacognition pertains to "thinking about thinking." Thus, the pupil looks back at facts, concepts, and generalizations acquired as well as skills achieved to ascertain their completeness. The pupil then notices :

- subject-matter lacking meaning,
- ideas which lack clarity,
- weaknesses in plans pertaining to a problem solving activity or a project which is in progress or completed,
- processes used in a discussion,
- improvements and refinements necessary in computer usage (Noddings, 2008).

Monitoring then has to do with evaluating if one is currently understanding sequential ideas within a learning activity. Reflecting deals with assessing content read or discussed, just recently. Metacognition emphasizes thinking about ideas and skills having been studied to ascertain what needs further elaboration.

Inservice Education

Social studies teachers must continually grow and develop professionally in teaching and learning. A professional library for teachers must be available in school, housing the latest in educational journals as well as teacher education textbooks. The internet must be accessible to teachers to view the latest in state and national journals in teaching social studies. Grade level meetings of social studies need to be encouraged whereby ideas may be shared. Workshops for social studies teachers need careful planning with vital topics being pursued. Teachers need to have opportunities to try out innovative ideas from the workshop in their own individual classrooms and report back to workshop members the success of the teaching endeavour (Sawchuk, 2008).

More inservice education opportunities are available to teachers than ever before. Online education makes it so that teachers may work at their own suitable time with no driving to distant places. Thus, inservice education may be done right in the home of the teacher. There are excellent online courses designed for social studies teachers. The times are indeed convenient for course taking.These need to meet personal teaching needs. Many accredited universities offer online graduate teacher education classes. Coursework also may be taken on a university campus leading to a graduate degree. Social studies teachers need to stay abreast of recent trends in teaching and learning. The psychology of teaching social studies needs to be given full attention such as engaging learners in each lesson and unit of study, pupils attaching meaning to ongoing activities as well as perceiving purpose in learning. From social science coursework, social studies teachers need to acquire structural ideas pertaining to each of the following academic disciplines useful in the preparation of lessons and units of study :

- history with relevant ideas dealing with the past. Primary sources are important to integrate into the curriculum.
- geography as it relates to place location, and how these relate to interaction with other regions
- political science with its emphasis upon laws, rules, and regulations, and their affect upon human beings
- economics including concepts such as goods, services, consumption, production, distribution, opportunity costs as well as advantages
- culture (anthropology and sociology) with the study of human inventions and institutions and their affect upon human behavior (Parker, 2001).

Each of the above need indepth study, analysis, meaning, and elaboration to improve teacher knowledge and skills in teaching the social studies. Quality attitudes should result toward the social studies curriculum and pupil achievement. Interest in computer use and technology is a motivating factor in staying abreast of what is current in teaching the social studies.

IN CONCLUSION

A Position Statement of the National Council for the Social Studies states the following pertaining to a "Vision of Powerful Teaching and Learning in the Social Studies," (2008):

- Key concepts and themes are developed in depth. The most effective social studies teachers do not diffuse their efforts by covering too many topics superficially. Breadth is important, but deep and thoughtful understanding is essential to prepare students for the issues of twenty-first century citizenship.
- Skills necessary to help our students thrive in a world of continuous and accelerated change are emphasized.

These include discipline based literacy, multicultural awareness, information gathering and analysis, inquiry and critical thinking, communication, data analysis, and the prudent use of 21st century media and technology. Skills are embedded throughout meaningful social studies lessons, rather than added on at the end.

- Teachers are reflective in planning, implementing, and assessing meaningful curriculum. Reflective teachers are well informed about the nature and purposes of social studies, have a continual, growing understanding of the disciplines that they teach, and keep up with pedagogical developments in the field of social studies.
- Meaningful curriculum includes extensive and reflective study of the United States and other nations' histories, religions, and cultures.

REFERENCES

Ediger, Marlow (2008), "Reading in the Social Studies," *Florida Council Social Studies Newsletter*, pp. 1-3.

Ediger, Marlow, and D. Bhaskara Rao (2000) *Teaching Social Studies Successfully*. New Delhi, India: Discovery Publishing House.

National Council for the Social Studies (2008), A Vision of Powerful Teaching and Learning in the Social Studies; Building Effective Citizens," *Social Education*, 72 (5), 277-278.

Noddings, Nel (2008), "All Our Students Thinking," *Educational Leadership*, 65 (5), 8-13.

National Council for the Social Studies (1994), *Curriculum Standards for the Social Studies*, Washington, DC: NCSS.

Parker, Walter C. (2000), *Social Studies in Elementary Education*. Merrill, Prentice-Hall: Upper Saddle River, New Jersey.

Rhodes, Joan A., and Tammy M. Milby (2007), "Teacher Created Electronic Books: Integrating Technology to Support Readers With Disabilities," *The Reading Teacher*, 61 (3), 255-259.

Sawchuk, Sean (September 10, 2008), Leadership Gap Seen in Post-NCLB Changes in U.S. Teachers," *Education Week*, 28 (3), 1, 16.

Constructivism in Social Studies

19

Constructivism, as a psychology of learning, needs to be studied and analyzed by teachers, supervisors, school administrators, as well as social studies educators. It might provide a strong basis for becoming in whole or in part a major tenet in teaching social studies.

With constructivism, the pupil is central in planning objectives, learning opportunities, and assessment procedures. Opposite of this method would be an adult determined social studies curriculum which might include measurably stated objectives, determined prior to instruction. Measuring and testing basically does not harmonize with constructivism. This tends to leave pupils out of becoming active participants in the social studies. Pupil input and questions are vital when learners are involved in sequencing their own experiences in the curriculum. What then might a constructivist social studies curriculum look like?

Teaching and Learning in the Social Studies

In an ongoing social studies unit of study, pupils need to be fully engaged in each ensuing lesson. When a unit is introduced, pupils may be involved in choosing problem areas for solving (Ediger and Rao, 2001). Thus, for example, in introducing a unit on The Middle East via a video tape, pupils may identify problems such as the following :

- Why is the land of Palestine called the Holy Land?
- Why is the walled city of Jerusalem holy to devout Muslims, Jews, and Christians?
- What is the importance of the cities of Hebron, Samaria (Nablus), Jericho, and Bethlehem?
- Which nations surround Israel and the West Bank and what importance is each in international affairs?

Once problems have been identified, pupils may volunteer to seek answers to identified problems areas. Three to four pupils may work to ascertain a solution to a problem. In planning to solve each problem, informations sources need to be selected and decisions made on the role of each pupil in doing the activity. Pupils individually must do their fair share of the work involved in finding a solution to an identified problem area. It is detrimental to any pupil who fails to achieve.

The teacher is a guide and facilitator, but does not tell pupils what and how to find answers to problems. He/she is well qualified in teaching the social studies with subject matter knowledge in the social sciences as well as in methods of teaching social studies. The social studies teacher then is efficient in offering suggestions where necessary, in order that pupils may make progress in ongoing units of study. Subject matter content and methodology is available to pupils in each ensuing lesson as resources, when needed (Ediger, 2007).

The teacher needs to continually upgrade teaching skills necessary to assist optimal learner achievement. Course work taken at an accredited university or taking quality courses online might well assist the teacher to stay abreast in his/her area of teaching specialization. Doing an independent study may further help the teacher to grow in knowledge and teaching skills. The independent study needs to emphasize indepth study as well as breadth of knowledge and skills. A professional library must have available textbooks and educational journals to help teachers grow professionally. Content gleaned needs to be discussed with peers and worthy ideas tried out in the classroom. What works should be shared with other teachers. How does a well prepared social studies teacher assist the psychology of constructivism in the classroom? He/she is better able to motivate pupils in learning by discovery whereby learners are engaged in decision making (Ediger, 2006).

Learning stations in the classroom are an important way to stress constructivism. Here, five or six stations may be set up, each containing approximately four tasks from which pupils individually may choose to complete. Choices might involve individual or committee endeavors. The stations pertain to different, relevant topics in the ongoing social studies unit of study such as a history, geography, economics, political science, and anthropology/sociology center. Materials and tools of instruction for pupil use need to be located at a central area in the classroom. Pupil choice in terms of what to learn and the means of learning are left up to the pupil. The teacher assists pupils as there is a need to do so. It is the pupil who does the learning and receives assistance from the teacher as necessary, in order to achieve sequential progress (Macy, 2004).

Project methods might well stress the psychology of constructivism in the social studies. Within an ongoing unit of study, pupils with teacher guidance volunteer/engage in doing a project. The project involves a construction activity and might, for example, involve making a model of the land of Palestine. Pupils need to study carefully a high quality map prior to doing the relief map. The relief map consisting of an equal mixture of flour and salt as well as enough water added to make a modeling paste. A map may be traced on plywood to show Israel and the West Bank with the modeling material placed thereon. The relief map might well show the following :

- the Sea of Galilee, approximately nine by thirteen miles in dimension, located ninety miles north/northeast of Jerusalem.
- the wavy Jordan River connecting the Sea of Galilee in the north with the Dead Sea in the south, a distance of 67 miles.
- the Dead Sea, approximately, thirteen by 46 miles in dimension.
- sea level may be shown with the Mediterranean Sea, located along the west coast.
- the Judean Hills go from the north end of the land of Palestine to Hebron in the south, a distance of approximately 100 miles. They vary in height, but generally are 2600 feet in elevation.

By constructing the relief map from modelling materials, pupils feel the elevation features and notice specifically each place being modeled. Important cities may be placed on the relief map. Kumran, the location of the Dead Sea scrolls, may be pinpointed on the relief map where the Dead Sea and the Jordan River join. Additional places may be added such as Tele Aviv, Nazareth, Caesarea, and Bethany, as well as the cities listed above under the first set of asterisks.

Using Basal Textbooks

Basal textbooks in an ongoing lesson/unit of study may harmonize well with constructivism as a psychology of teaching. It is essential that pupils have adequate background information to benefit from the ensuing reading activity. The related illustrations in the text might well be used to provide these background experiences. Thus, pupils may raise questions pertaining to the pictures such as the following on the Middle East :

- Why is the Dome of the Rock, a Muslim Mosque, important to devout Arabs.
- How does the Jewish Wailing Wall fit into their recorded history?
- Why is the Church of the Holy Sepulcher salient to people of the Christian religion?
- Why were the Crusades fought during the Middle Ages?

The new words may be identified by pupils and their textual meaning discussed as they are viewed individually from the chalkboard. Learners then should be ready to read from the ensuing textbook content. As they read, pupils may seek answers to the identified questions. Following the silent reading, pupils with teacher guidance for the class as a whole, or within small groups, may discuss answers to identified questions. Critical and creative thinking are to be encouraged. Additional reference sources may be needed to seek information. Internet sources, among others, are valuable to use. Pupils need to raise questions at any time. Curiosity and interest are important (Barth, 2006).

Sustained silent reading harmonizes well with the social studies curriculum. The teacher, here, needs to select library books which are directly related to the ongoing social studies unit being taught. These books must be on a variety of reading levels and genera to provide for individual differences. Each may then choose an appropriate book to read which is on his/her reading level. The teacher observes to notice if pupils individually are actively engaged in reading. The teacher intervenes and chooses a library book for a child to read, if the latter cannot settle down in reading sequential library books.

IN CLOSING

The constructivist psychology of teaching and learning may well be summarized with the following conclusions pertaining to teacher respect of pupils in the following areas :

- using student's interest in class activities.
- allowing students to express ideas without criticism.
- correcting errors without putdowns.
- balancing corrective feedback with recognition of strengths.
- displaying student products, and.
- using specific praise (Stronge, 2002).

A teacher displays courtesy by

- smiling often.
- being positive.
- not interrupting.
- exhibiting simple politeness such as picking up up a dropped item, or holding a door.
- greeting students when they arrive and wishing them well when they leave (Mawhinney and Sagan, 2007).

Placing the learner at the center of curriculum planning is salient in developing a constructivist psychology of instruction.

REFERENCES

Earth, Roland (2006), "Improving Relationships Within the Schoolhouse," *Educational Leadership*, 63 (6), 6-13.

Ediger, Marlow (2007), "Teacher Observation to Evaluate Achievement," *Journal of Instructional Psychology*, 34 (3),137-139.

Ediger, Marlow (1006), "Administration of Schools," *College Student Journal*, 40 (4), 846-851.

Ediger, Marlow, and D. Bhaskara Rao (2001), *Teaching Social Studies Successfully*. New Delhi, India : Discovery Publishing House.

Macy, Leonora (2004), "A Novel Study Through Drama," *The Reading Teacher*, 58 (3), 240- 249.

Mawhinney, Thomas S., and Laura L. Sagan (2007), "The Power of Personal Relationships," *Phi Delta Kappan*, 88 (6), p 463.

Stronge, James H. (2002), *Qualities of Effective Teachers*. Alexandria, Virginia: Association for Supervision and Curriculum Development.

Psychology of Teaching Social Studies

20

A perennial question for social studies teachers is how to secure maximum achievement from students. Students need to attain optimally within their own developmental level. The psychology of learning and its uses may well assist teachers in teaching and learning situations. There are specific educational psychologies which might well guide student progress in the social studies.

The Psychology of Learning and the Social Studies

Motivated learners is a key consideration in assisting students to achieve objectives of instruction. The motivated learner does well in the social studies. There are several considerations to consider here. First, the learning styles of students need to be studied and provisions for these must be made. Selected students prefer a more structured learning environment than do others. Here, Social Studies Teacher A chooses the objectives for learners to attain. Learning experiences for students to achieve these ends are also selected by the teacher. The following steps are then followed by the teacher in teaching students :

- choosing and sequencing each activity carefully
- maintaining student on task behavior
- observing achievement in the ongoing lesson and unit of study

- using teacher made and mandated tests to measure achievement
- evaluating test results to be used for diagnosis and remediation purposes (Ediger and Rao, 2001).

The teacher, here, uses voice inflection to obtain learner attention, but believes in instruction being conveyed from teacher to student. Time is valuable and the teacher has considerable ground to cover in teaching and a no-nonsense, polite method of instruction best helps students to learn optimally. A quiet classroom environment is in evidence. Praise is given at intervals to motivate achievement. Inexpensive prizes are given for learner achievement. The latter is given for good test results. Even though, considerable subject matter is to be taught, indepth teaching is still emphasized of salient social studies concepts and generalizations.

Teacher A believes strongly in deductive instruction in motivating learners in teaching/learner activities. Extrinsic motivation is the key to good student achievement in the social studies (Ediger, 2005).

In contrast, Social Studies Teacher B is quite flexible in stressing openness in the classroom environment. Students are to feel relaxed in teaching and learning situations. They feel free to ask questions and make comments directly related to the ongoing lesson. There is laughter involving students and the teacher when humorous incidents occur in the classroom. When initiating a new social studies unit, Teacher B :

- provides readiness activities for learners. This may be done by having students view a related video tape. Additional learning activities may be used as readiness experiences as needed. Students are encouraged to raise questions resulting in problems to be solved in the ongoing unit of study.
- assists students to list and clarify new vocabulary terms to be encountered in ongoing learning opportunities.

- encourages learner input into suggesting personal projects to be developed.
- emphasizes freedom of movement by students when getting supplies and materials in the classroom. This results in a busy classroom with some necessary noise.
- the use of a variety of learning activities as the unit of study progresses such as cooperative work and individual endeavors.
- varied evaluation techniques used to appraise student achievement and progress. Students are rather heavily involved in appraising their own progress, including self evaluation (Lent, 2006).

Teacher B believes strongly in intrinsic motivation when assisting learners in the classroom in the ongoing social studies unit of study. Both teachers have justifications in using the philosophy of instruction which promotes optimal progress among learners. Perhaps, this may be resolved when viewing styles of learning possessed by students. Some students may prefer a more structured learning environment than others. Thus, there are students who prefer more of concrete and semi-concrete learning activities than those desiring abstract experiences. Students may prefer objects and realia, as well as pictorial forms of learning as compared to those emphasizing reading and writing experiences, solely or largely (Ediger, 2007).

Additional learning opportunities in the social studies include deductive versus inductive experiences. How much of each is used will come in degrees for learners. Deductive experiences stress explanations and comments of subject matter to students who then in return practice the use of the obtained knowledge in a plethora of ways. In each social studies unit, there are salient facts, concepts, and generalizations which need clarification to students. For example, a brief explanation here, may stress the ownership of the fief by the lord. Also, an explanation of lord's mill for grinding grain might well be given orally as well as of peasant life. Evaluation of achievement may follow with responses students give to questions asked by the teacher pertaining to the manor including its mill operations and of peasant life (Brown, 2006).

Inductive learning stresses problems and hypotheses identified by students in an ongoing lesson. Students are then guided to secure answers to these problems as well as test each hypothesis. A variety of reference sources may be used here such as the internet, the basal textbook, and library books among others. When attending a National Council for the Social convention, a presenter in a meeting said he never answered questions of students directly, but rather asked related questions anew, leading the learner to think through the answer to the problem. Thus, for example, instead of explaining the role of the lord and his mill as well as peasant life on the manor, the social studies teacher would assist learners to locate materials to determine possible answers as well as test hypotheses. Inductive thinking is then involved.

To indicate what has been learned in the social studies, selected students may prefer a paper pencil test consisting of multiple choice and/or essay test items. Multiple choice test items might be preferred by the student due to it being machine scored or checked with an answer sheet and being "objective". Essay responses involve more subjectivity in grading; however, a well developed rubric assists in obtaining more objectivity in scoring.

Other students may prefer a more open ended procedure of assessment. Instead of testing, students individually or collectively may indicate learnings achieved through :

- doing a mural on a selected topic dealing with the Middle Ages period of time. Here, students may do a mural on noblemen engaging in battle to obtain more land, including other manors.

- writing diverse forms of poetry involving what had been studied.
- engaging in creative or formal dramatizations for classmates to observe. This may stress three stages in becoming a guild member an apprentice, journeyman, and master. These stages indicate what is required in each level to becoming a guild member. Masters produced excellence in products produced at what was deemed a fair price.
- doing illustrations for a bound paperback. Subject-matter written by students should accompany each illustration. These drawings and accompanying subject matter might deal with the three stages of becoming a knight such as being a page, a squire, and then knighthood.
- Learning centres in which students may choose sequential tasks to complete from a task card located at each center (Niles, 2007).

Student/teacher planning may be used to evaluate each of the above. Included in the plans should be clearly defined criteria to be used in the assessment procedure for each completed product.

IN CLOSING

The writer has indicated two somewhat opposite strategies for teaching social studies. Comparisons were then made between rather highly structured sequences and considerably more open ended processes to be used in teaching and learning situations. Most teachers tend to be somewhat in between the two approaches when selecting objectives, learning opportunities, and appraisal procedures. The important aim in teaching the social studies is to help each student to attain as optimally as possible. Students do differ in learning styles possessed. The following guidelines, used by teachers in teaching, should assist in aiding learner progress :

- engaging students in active involvement in ongoing learning opportunities.
- helping students perceive purpose or reasons for participating in the curriculum.
- guiding students to sense meaning in what is being learned.
- stressing critical and creative thinking as well as problem solving n ongoing lessons and units of study.
- developing needed skills to comprehend subject matter while reading.
- using technology, such as the internet, to secure necessary information.
- providing for individual differences among learners.

REFERENCES

Brown, Dennis (June, 2006), "Motivation Efforts on Standardized Tests," *Iowa Educational Leadership*, 8 (4), 14-19.

Ediger, Marlow (2005), "Present Day Philosophies of Education," *Journal of Instructional Psychology*, 33 (3), 179-182.

Ediger, Marlow, (2007), "Learning Activities in the Curriculum," *College Student Journal*, 41 (4), 967-969.

Ediger, Marlow, and D. Bhaskara Rao (2001), *Teaching Social Studies Successfully*. New Delhi, India: Discovery Publishing House.

Lent, ReLeah (2006), "In the Company of Critical Thinkers," *Educational Leadership* 64 (2), 68-73.

Ness, Molly (2007), "Reading Comprehension Strategies in Secondary Area Classrooms." *Phi Delta Kappa,* 89 (3), 229-231.

21 No Child Left Behind (NCLB) and Social Studies

No Child Left Behind does does not require measuring pupil achievement in the social studies. It does have requirements for pupils to pass mandated tests in grades three though eight, covering reading and mathematics, as well as science. An exit test is mandated for students in high school. Not only is social studies left out from required testing, but also music, art, and physical education in grades three through eight. The NCLB has greatly limited the scope of what will be tested. What will be tested is usually what receives major emphasis in the curriculum. Reports from different school systems indicate that teachers spend much time in drilling students on subject-matter which might appear on NCLB tests, than on the non-tested curriculum. In addition to pupils passing tests to be promoted to the next higher grade level and passing an exit, adequate yearly progress must show the level of proficiency by the 2013 school year. Many school systems indicate that their pupils cannot achieve at that designated level. This means that social studies will/might continue to be omitted or minimized in the school curriculum (Barton, 2006).

This chapter will deal with stressing the social studies in classrooms despite it being omitted by NCLB for testing purposes. Suffice it to say that selected school systems test in the social studies as a local school policy.

Emphasizing the Social Studies

This manuscript will then relate to social studies being taught formally, informally or in relationship to other curriculum areas. In teaching the social studies as a separate academic discipline, teachers need to state relevant objectives clearly, so that it can be understood what will be taught. Three categories of objectives need to be emphasized—the first kind is knowledge ends. Here, the teacher needs to choose significant objectives which are useful in school and in society. Vital facts, concepts, and generalizations should be emphasized in teaching and learning situations. Careful selection of these knowledge objectives is important. There is much for pupils to learn and each objective must have much merit (Ediger and Rao, 2002).

A second kind of objective to stress in teaching is skills ends. With skills, pupils use what is being learned as knowledge. Skills may be acquired through critical thinking. Here, the pupil separates facts from opinions, fantasy from reality, as well as accurate from inaccurate content. Analyzing assists pupils to use knowledge in different ways such as in problem solving. A related skill is creative thinking whereby the pupil uses subject matter to come up with unique ideas. These novel ideas stress originality. The pupil then is motivated to come up with a new product, process, or approach in solving problem areas. Project methods also emphasize originality in construction or art work as it is related to the ongoing social studies unit of study (Ediger, 2008).

A third kind of objective stresses the attitudinal dimension. Attitudes are feelings the learner acquires as a result of teaching and learning experiences. They are vital ends when getting along well with others. The following are salient attitudes :

- treating others fairly and with consideration.
- working harmoniously in small and large groups.
- eliminating rude and impolite behaviour.
- being a caring person.
- having a good attitude toward the curriculum and toward learning in general (Ediger, 2008).

The Informal Social Studies Curriculum

Many of the above named objectives for a formal social studies curriculum are vital, too, in informal learnings, such as "having a good attitude toward the curriculum and learning in general." If social studies is being minimized in many schools, there are still a variety of interesting activities which provide needed pupil learnings in attitudinal development. Reading aloud to pupils during story time might well involve salient expository library books to develop quality attitudes, among other objectives of instruction. For example, there are a plethora of biographical books about statesmen, inventors, leaders of nations, and industrialists, among everyday individuals in society. Reading aloud from these library books with proper stress, pitch, and voice inflection, the teacher may engage pupils actively in listening to important ideas from the social studies. Questions may be asked by listeners involving critical and creative thinking. Questioning the Author (QtA) emphasizes that the writer is not infallible and many vital questions may be asked of the subject matter, including its accuracy. Reciprocal teaching (Palincsar and Brown, 1984) may be used to evaluate comprehension from orally read materials by asking students to summarize, question, clarify, and predict from the text. The teacher, too, may ask relevant questions pertaining to content read.

The questions may pertain to the following :

- what do you think is the main idea the writer presented? Readiness always needs to be inherent on the learner's part and in this case having definite knowledge/skills of what a main idea is.

- which content provides information to support the main idea?
- have you experienced something like this in your own life?

In addition to the teacher read aloud, peers may also interact with each other in taking turns when reading orally. Three or four students may take turns in a read aloud. The social studies subject-matter needs to be engaging when peers read orally. They may choose their own questions and problem areas to discuss. Vygotsky (1978) advocated pupils working together in small groups with ideas circulating among peers so that higher levels of cognition were possible. Ideas presented would assist pupils to attain more complex ideas through scaffolding. Thus, an idea may be too difficult to understand, but in smaller sequential steps, the complex ideas may be achieved. Ideas "bounce" off the minds of pupils as scaffolds to achieve more complicated ideas.

What is read may lend itself to further interpretation of subject-matter. Thus, a creative dramatics presentation may be developed whereby each student has a role to play. The assigned or voluntary part must be thoroughly familiar to the presenter. This means reading and rereading the part accepted by the role player to do well in the creative dramatics presentation. Each role is to be performed without the script being available or present. Visitors may be invited to view the informal creative dramatics activity, including parents and pupils from other classrooms (Ediger, 2008).

Bulletin Board Displays and Individualized Reading

Change in bulletin board displays should occur before pupils lose interest in its contents. The teacher may observe the frequency of pupils viewing the bulletin board to notice when a new display is needed. A variety of kinds of displays need to be in the offing. Thus, attractive library book jackets with an appealing caption might well attract learner attention. The bulletin board may be used to entice pupil interests in reading these books. The teacher also needs to introduce each book by telling a few interesting ideas about their contents. When supervising university student teachers in the public schools, the writer noticed either the cooperating or student teacher briefly tell, enthusiastically, about a children's book, he/she had read. Pupils generally read these same library books to themselves. It is good to set a period of time aside each day for independent reading during the school hours. Self-selection of social studies books, located at a reading center, should make it possible for a pupil to find a title of suitable difficulty to read on his/her own. Enjoyment in reading library books should be an end result. Encouragement needs to be given to all pupils to read , during the recreational reading time. Time may be given in class to share information read (Gomez and Gomez, 2007). There are a plethora of objectives which pupils may achieve in the time devoted to individualized reading :

- pupil knowledge in the social studies should increase.
- pupil attitudes toward reading and the social studies should be favorable. Positive attitudes assist in wanting to do more reading.
- pupil skills in reading content may transfer to other academic areas.

There may be opportunities to have pupil/teacher conferences pertaining to library books read. The conference might well include a few questions to ask of pupils covering the contents of the completed library book read. Learners may also be asked to read several paragraphs aloud to check progress in reading fluency. Brief, dated notes may be made of the completed conference. These notes may be referred to when conducting another conference with the same pupil (Ediger, 2008).

To facilitate quality silent reading endeavours, the teacher or a peer may assist those who need help in word recognition. A good reader might read to others in a small group setting to encourage interest in subject matter content in the social studies. Selected books may have accompanying audios to help readers comprehend as well as learn to identify unknown words,Then too, social studies library books may be taken home for reading. Schools need to stress reading achievement wherever possible. During parent/teacher conferences, the importance of reading aloud to children must be emphasized. It is excellent to discuss with parents what pupils are reading at home. This includes books checked out from the school library as well as those provided by the home. With young children, reading aloud should be emphasized, using proper standards. E-mail messages may be sent from parents to the teacher on pupil home reading habits. The teacher may also respond to the e-mail, as well as suggest library books to read. Open channels of communication need to be stressed (Petress, 2006).

The Academic Disciplines and the Social Studies

Social studies library books contain content on the different disciplines comprising the social studies. There are numerous children library books on history, geography, political science (government), culture (anthropology and sociology), and economics. Rodgers *et al.* (2007) list library book titles containing the following fundamental economic concepts: goods and services, savings, money/banking, opportunity cost, producers/consumers, savings, scarcity, wants/needs, profit, strikes, among others. Practical application may be made by pupils pertaining to each of the above named concepts :

- pupils may name which goods and services they need almost every day
- if they have money saved, this can be discussed

- money might be named in terms of coins and bills. The teacher may show an example of each to children as they are being discussed.
- opportunity costs may be explained in terms of advantages and disadvantages of each job or vocation being discussed.
- producers (those who provide the needed goods and services) and consumers (those who buy and use the needed goods and services for everyday living).
- scarcity pertains to a valuable resource of which a limited amount is available.
- wants (those things a person would like to have and purchase) and needs (what a person truly must have and buy to live).
- profit pertains to earnings of a company for taking risks in the business world.

The above underlined are a few of the economic concepts, among others, from economics, as an academic discipline. They are relevant for pupils to learn in an informal or formal social studies curriculum. Salient concepts from diverse academic disciplines need to be studied by pupils, sequenced meaningfully, so they may be achieved by pupils. Each concept must be elaborated upon and made useful for learners. Concrete, semi-concrete, and abstract experiences are necessary for pupils so that learnings become purposeful, significant, and understandable.

REFERENCES

Barton, Paul E. (2006), "Needed Higher Standards in Accountability," *Educational Leadership*, 64 (3), 28-31.

Ediger, Marlow (2008a), "Current Events, the Student, and the Social Studies", *Social Studies Review*, 47 (2), 58-60.

Ediger, Marlow (2008b), "Mental Health in the Classroom," *Journal of Instructional Psychology*, 35 (1), 38-42.

Ediger, Marlow (2008c), "The Old Order Amish and the Social Studies," *Perspectives*, 38 (4), 13-16.

Ediger, Marlow (2008d), "The School Principal as Reading Supervisor," *Reading Improvement*, 45 (3), 153-156.

Ediger, Marlow, and D. Bhaskara Rao (2002), *Teaching Social Social. Studies Successfully*. New Delhi, India: Discovery Publishing House.

Gomez, Lewis M., and Kimberely Gomez (2007), "Reading for Learning: Literacy Supports for 21st Century Work," *Phi Delta Kappan*, 89 (3), 224-228.

Palincsar, A. S., and A. L. Brown (1984), "Reciprocal Teaching of Comprehension-fostering and Comprehension-monitoring Activities," *Cognition and Instruction*, 1 (2),117-175.

Petress (2006), "An Operational Definition of Class Participation," College Student Journal, 40 (4), 821-823.

Rodgers, Yana V. *et al.* (2007), "Teaching Economic Concepts Through Children Literature in the Primary Grades," *The Reading Teacher*, 61 (1), 46-55.

Vygotsky, L. S. (1978), Mind In Society: *The Development of Higher Psychological Processes*. Cambridge, Massachusetts: Harvard University Press.

Data Driven Decision in Making in Social Studies

22

Data driven decision making emphasizes the importance of the teacher using objective sources of information in developing the social studies curriculum. Too frequently, decisions of teachers have been made based on routine and outdated methods of teaching. Valid and reliable tests used to secure results from pupil learning make for better selection of objectives, learning opportunities, and appraisal procedures. Pupils must make continuous progress in ongoing lessons and units of study in the social studies. Teacher use of data provides opportunities in making for quality pupil sequence in the social studies.

Securing Data

Tests used to evaluate pupil academic achievement must be valid in that they measure accurately in the respective academic discipline. Thus, a social studies test must measure pupil knowledge in this academic field. The test also needs to measure consistently so that the teacher has precise knowledge of what the pupil knows in the social studies. Reliability may consist of test/retest, alternative forms, and/or split half reliability. The objectives for each test should be available to social studies teachers for use in teaching and learning situations. This makes for greater validity in teaching as compared to pupils being tested on unfamiliar subject matter.

Pupil standardized test results need to provide an overview of a learner's overall achievement as compared to others in the norm group upon which the test was standardized. Thus, percentite ranks, grade equivalent, and stanines are given in the Manual which may then be matched with each pupil's test results in the social studies. It must be realized that pupils differ from each other in a plethora of ways including abilities possessed, intelligence, and motivation. Of utmost importance is to compare how well the pupil did as compared to previous test results. Each pupil should make optimal progress from one testing to the other. Teachers need to have test results pertaining to which test items were missed by the learner. He/she might then plan how each pupil may achieve more optimally in the social studies by basing instruction on test items missed.

The test item missed should have broad implications for teaching social studies, not narrow factual information. The broad implications include concepts, generalizations, and main ideas. These may be tested in ensuing learning opportunities and are useful in many situations, in school and in society (Ediger, 2008).

Standardized tests are generally given once a year and comparisons for each pupil may be made in achievement from one year to the next. In the mean time, teacher written tests, properly crafted, may provide valuable feedback on learner progress. These test should also be valid. The teacher of social studies may write a multiple choice test item as he/she teaches a concept, generalization, and/or main idea. Face validity is then being stressed. It is not good to ask test questions for which pupils have had tittle/no previous opportunity for learning. These test items lack validity. In writing each multiple choice test item, the social studies teacher needs to :

- write a stem (not all have stems) which harmonizes grammatically with four distractors.
- write distractors which are all plausible. The following is not a plausible distractor: The first president of the United States was (*a*) Mickey Mouse.
- write distractors of similar length so as not to provide clues as to which is the correct (or incorrect) answer.
- provide no clues in writing as to which is the correct response such as : The capitol cities of Saudi Arabia are (*a*) Riyad and Mecca, (*b*) Ammon, (*c*) Damascus, (*d*) Baghdad.

By developing high quality tests, the teacher has a much better opportunity of obtaining relevant data for social studies curricular decision-making. If test items are poorly written, the teacher has little to go by in improving social studies instruction (Ediger, 2008).

True/false test items have merit in evaluating pupils achievement if they attempt to eliminate the possibility of excessive guessing, otherwise the pupil has a fifty percent chance of guessing correct responses. Notice the following true/false test item: The Sea of Galilee is the largest body of water in the land of Palestine. The answer is false. The pupil needs to change what is false to make the previous statement true. Thus, *The Dead Sea* is the largest body of water in the land of Palestine.

Matching test items in the social studies, carefully written by the teacher, provide information from test results for teaching and learning situations. Multiple choice test items need to follow the following criteria :

- there should be more items in one column than the other in order to minimize the process of elimination to come up with correct answers. It is always good to match known items in column A with the correct response in column B first, then the remainder has a few extra items to avoid guessing which is correct.

The teacher desires to have accurate, relevant information from test results in order to improve sequence and accuracy of knowledge.

- one of the two columns should have words or short phrases only, not complete sentences. It becomes exceedingly complex if both columns for matching have complete sentences.
- the written matching test should harmonize with the developmental level of the test taker. Thus, the test may be too lengthy or too short depending upon the mental maturity level of the pupil. Words used must be on the understanding level of test takers (See Burke 2005).

Essay tests written by the teacher provide opportunities for pupils to organizing ideas, sequence written content, as well as indicate breadth and depth in learning. Clarity of ideas expressed is of utmost importance which must be meaningful to the reader of the essay test items. The pupil, here, is attempting to communicate content in writing. If long hand is used, then quality handwriting needs to be emphasized. Additional mechanics in written work include proper punctuation, grammar, letter formation, capitalization of words, and as well as alignment of letters and words. Essay test items need to adhere to the following standards :

- be on the developmental level of the involved learners
- be valid and aligned with the objectives of the lesson/ unit of study
- be meaningfully written so that pupils know what is wanted in terms of responses
- be written so that creative and critical thinking, as well as problem solving are stressed
- be evaluated with quality rubric assistance. Rubric results can emphasize interscorer reliability if several evaluate the same essays using the criteria in the rubric (Ediger, 2007).

With teacher written tests, pupils have opportunities to reveal intrinsically what has been accomplished and the resulting information may be highly useful to pinpoint specifics in what is left to learn. These test items truly reflect what is taught in a unit of study.

They may not possess the validity and reliability inherent in pilot studied and analyzed standardized tests, also called norm referenced tests distinguishable from criterion referenced tests.

To improve unit teaching in the social studies, the teacher must secure vital test information from pupils. *Formative* evaluation stresses the importance of securing information of pupil learning along the way when the unit is implemented. This gives chances for the teacher to make revisions and modifications before the unit ends. Thus, from feedback obtained, the teacher may make necessary changes in objectives to be emphasized in teaching, learning activities to achieve these objectives, as well as the appraisal procedures themselves.

Summative evaluation emphasizes end of unit appraisal. When the social studies unit has been completed, the teacher views test results from summative evaluation. Here, in reviewing the data, the social studies teacher attempts to answer the following :

- which changes should be made in the unit of study for the next school year?
- what modifications need to be made in the objectives, the learning opportunities, as well as the appraisal procedures?
- which grouping procedures, if any, in the classroom should be changed?
- how much stress needs to be placed upon individual versus cooperative endeavors in learning?
- should enrichment activities be included as motivators for learning? (See National Council for the Social Studies, 2008).

There are schools and teachers who emphasize benchmarks in achievement. Thus, there are goals which learners need to achieve within a unit at an approximate time. The social studies teacher may then evaluate what pupils have accomplished and what is left to learn. This is a time for reflection and further planning to optimize learner achievement.

There are cautions to observe in testing pupils. These include the following :

- pupils may be tested too frequently, especially when other methods of appraisal are useful such as teacher observation of pupil achievement. Adequate time must be available for instruction, also.
- pupils may refrain from putting forth effort in test taking if too many are given.
- there are a plethora of additional methods to determine what pupils have learned, than standardized and other forms of paper/pencil tests.
- pupil fatigue may set in with too many tests to taken.

There are plethora of additional methods to use in appraising learner achievement, than testing. These include the following in the social studies :

- teacher observation, briefly referred to above. Here, the social studies teacher may notice immediately where a pupil needs more assistance. Thus, a pupil may need help with understanding and drawing lines of latitude and longitude in geography.
- discussion settings in which learners reveal they do not attach meaning to the concepts of time in history as in the French Revolution related to other events in context. Assistance might well then be provided for pupils to develop greater insights into this period of time.
- a debate involving governmental intervention versus the free enterprise system in health care provisions, in the political science and economics domain.

- a chart developed within a committee to show the influence of culture on human behavior (Ahmad (2009).

Somewhat opposite of measurement psychology of instruction is constructivism. Constructivism emphasizes the following :

- a pupil centered approach in teaching whereby they are actively involved in the instructional arena
- pupil/teacher planning of objectives, learning activities, and evaluation procedures
- pupils sequence their own individual learnings
- pupils with teacher guidance learn by discovery methods
- testing is greatly minimized. Teacher observation and pupil self evaluation are used in assessment.

REFERENCES

Ahmad, Sajjad (2009), "Evolving A Framework for Teaching and Learning," *Edutracks*, 8 (9), 11-12.

Burke, Karen (2005), "Teacher Certification Exams: What Are the Predictors of Success?" *College Student Journal*, 39 (4), 784-793.

Ediger, Marlow (2007), "Teacher Observation to Assess Student Achievement," *Journal of Instructional Psychology*, 34 (3),137-139.

Ediger, Marlow (2008a), "Leadership in the School Setting," *Education*, 129 (1), 17-20.

Ediger, Marlow (2008), "The School and Students in Society," *Journal* of *Instructional Psychology*, 35 (3), 260-263.

National Council for the Social Studies (2008), "A Vision of Powerful Teaching and Learning in the Social Studies: Building Effective Citizens," *Social Education*, 72 (5), 277-280.

Additional Reading

Amala, P. A. and Anupama, P., Authors and Digumarti Bhaskara Rao, Editor (2004). *History of Education.* New Delhi : Discovery Publishing House. ISBN 81-7141-860-0.

Appala Naidu, P.Ch., Author and Digumarti Bhaskara Rao, Editor (2007). *Student Feedback Methods.* New Delhi : Discovery Publishing House.

Bhaskara Rao, Digumarti (1994). *Scientific Aptitude.* New Delhi : Ashish Publishing House. ISBN 81-7024-658-X.

Bhaskara Rao, Digumarti (1995). *Animal Kingdom.* New Delhi : Discovery Publishing House. ISBN 81-7141-274-2.

Bhaskara Rao, Digumarti (1995). *Batracology.* New Delhi : Discovery Publishing House. ISBN 81-7141-279-3.

Bhaskara Rao, Digumarti (1997). *Scientific Attitude.* New Delhi : Discovery Publishing House. ISBN 81-7141-381-1.

Bhaskara Rao, Digumarti (1996). *Scientific Attitude vis-à-vis Scientific Aptitude.* New Delhi : Discovery Publishing House. ISBN 81-7141-308-0.

Bhaskara Rao, Digumarti (2004). *Scientific Attitude, Scientific Aptitude and Achievement.* New Delhi : Discovery Publishing House. ISBN 81-7141-781-7.

Bhaskara Rao, Digumarti (2004). *Educational Administration.* New Delhi : Discovery Publishing House. ISBN 81-7141-842-2.

Bhaskara Rao, Digumarti (2004). *Issues in School Education.* New Delhi : Discovery Publishing House. ISBN 81-8356-025-3.

Bhaskara Rao, Digumarti, Editor (1996). *Encyclopaedia of Education For All,* 5 Volumes. New Delhi : APH Publishing Corporation. ISBN 81-7024-759-4 (set).

Vol. I *Education For All : The World Conference.* ISBN 81-7024-760-8

Vol. II *Education For All : The EPA-9 Summit.* ISBN 81-7024-761-6

Vol. II *Education For All : Quality Education For All*. ISBN 81-7024-762-6.

Vol. IV *Education For All : Planning and Monitoring*. ISBN 81-7024-763-4.

Vol. V *Education For All : The Indian Scenario*. ISBN 81-7024-764-0.

Bhaskara Rao, Digumarti, Editor (1999). *International Encyclopaedia of AIDS*, 11 Volumes. New Delhi: Discovery Publishing House. ISBN 81-7141-522-6 (set).

Vol. 1 *Introduction to HIV/AIDS*. ISBN 81-7141-523-7.

Vol. 2 *HIV/AIDS – Issues and Challenges*, 2 parts. ISBN 81-7141-524-5.

Vol. 3 *HIV/AIDS – Socio Economic Realities*. ISBN 81-7141-524-3.

Vol. 4 *HIV/AIDS – Law Ethics and Human Rights*, 2 parts. ISBN 81-7141-526-1.

Vol. 5 *AIDS and NGOs*. ISBN 81-7141-527-X.

Vol. 6 *AIDS and Home Care*. ISBN 81-7141-528-8.

Vol. 7 *STD Case Management*. ISBN 81-7141-529-6.

Vol. 8 *HIV/AIDS Prevention and Care – Teaching Modules for Nurses and Midwives*. ISBN 81-7141-530-X.

Vol. 9 *HIV Prevention Education for Educational Institutions*. ISBN 81-7141-531-8.

Vol.10 *Instructional Modules for AIDS Education*. ISBN 81-7141-532-6.

Vol.11 *School Health Education to prevent AIDS and STD – A Package for Curriculum Planners*. ISBN 81-7141-533-4.

Bhaskara Rao, Digumarti, Editor (2000). *International Encyclopaedia of Human Rights*, 7 volumes in 13 parts. New Delhi : Discovery Publishing House. ISBN 81-7141-567-9 (set).

Vol. 1 *International Instruments of Human Rights*, 2 parts. ISBN 81-7141-569-4.

Vol. 2 *Regional Instruments of Human Rights*. ISBN 81-7141-604-7.

Vol. 3 *Human Rights and the United Nations*, 2 parts. ISBN 81-7141-605-5.

Vol. 4 *Fact Files of Human Rights*, 3 parts. ISBN 81-7141-606-3.

Vol. 5 *Study Stories of Human Rights*, 3 parts. ISBN 81-7141-607-3.

Vol. 6 *International Meetings on Human Rights*, 2 parts. ISBN 81-714-608-X.

Vol. 7 *Professional Training in Human Rights*. ISBN 81-7141-609-8.

Bhaskara Rao, Digumarti, Editor (2000). *International Encyclopaedia of Science and Technology Education,* 11 Volumes. New Delhi : Discovery Publishing House. ISBN 81-7141-548-2 (set).

Vol. 1 *Science and Technology Education.* ISBN 81-7141-568-7.

Vol. 2 *Science Education in Developing Countries.* ISBN 81-7141-569-9.

Vol. 3 *Organizational Structure of Science.* ISBN 81-7141-570-9.

Vol. 4 *Science Education in Asia and the Pacific.* ISBN 81-7141-571-7

Vol. 5 *Science and Technology Education For All.* ISBN 81-7141-572-5.

Vol. 6 *Values, Ethics, Talent and Girls in Science and Technology Education.* ISBN 81-7141-573-3.

Vol. 7 *Popularization of Science and Technology Education.* ISBN 81-7141-574-1.

Vol. 8 *Science, Power and Society.* ISBN 81-7141- 575-X.

Vol. 9 *Information Technology.* ISBN 81-7141-576-8.

Vol.10 *Teacher Training in Science and Technology Education.* ISBN 81-7142-577-6.

Vol.11 *Teacher Training in Science and Technology: A Curriculum Framework.* ISBN 81-7141-578-4.

Bhaskara Rao, Digumarti, Editor (2000). *Education For All : Achieving the Goal,* 3 volumes. New Delhi : APH Publishing Corporation. ISBN 81-7648-152-1 (set).

Vol. I *The Global Consensus.* ISBN 81-7648-155-6.

Vol. II *Mid-Decade Review Reports of Regional Seminars.* ISBN 81-7648-154-8.

Vol. III *Issues and Trends.* ISBN 81-7648-155-6.

Bhaskara Rao, Digumarti, Editor (2004). *International Encyclopaedia of Learning to Live Together,* 4 Volumes. New Delhi : Discovery Publishing House. ISBN 81-7141-848-1.

Vol. 1 *International Conference on Learning to Live Together.*

Vol. 2 *Globalization and Living Together.*

Vol. 3 *Curriculum for Learning to Live Together.*

Vol. 4 *Science Education for the Contemporary Society .*

Bhaskara Rao, Digumarti, Editor (2005). *Encyclopaedia of Education For All,* 3 Volumes. New Delhi : Discovery Publishing House. ISBN 81-7141-647-0 (set).

Bhaskara Rao, Digumarti, Editor (2007). *Encyclopaedia of Teacher Education,* 4 Volumes. New Delhi : Discovery Publishing House. ISBN 81-8356-306-6 (set).

Bhaskara Rao, Digumarti, Editor (2007). *Encyclopaedia of Education for Living Together*, 4 Volumes. New Delhi : Discovery Publishing House. ISBN 81-7141-848-1 (set).

Bhaskara Rao, Digumarti, Editor (1996). *National Policy on Education*, 2 Volumes. New Delhi: Anmol Publications Pvt. Ltd. ISBN 81-7488-323-1.

Bhaskara Rao, Digumarti, Editor (1996). *Global Perceptions on Peace Education*, 3 Volumes. New Delhi : Discovery Publishing House. ISBN 81-7141-319-6.

Bhaskara Rao, Digumarti, Editor (1997). *Education for the 21st Century.* New Delhi : Discovery Publishing House. ISBN 81-7141-389-7.

Bhaskara Rao, Digumarti, Editor (1997). *Reflections on Scientific Attitude.* New Delhi : Discovery Publishing House. ISBN 81-7141-319-6.

Bhaskara Rao, Digumarti, Editor (1997). *Success Story of a Primary Education Project.* New Delhi : APH Publishing Corporation. ISBN 81-7024-850-7.

Bhaskara Rao, Digumarti, Editor (1997). *World Food Summit.* New Delhi : Discovery Publishing House. ISBN 81-7141-386-2.

Bhaskara Rao, Digumarti, Editor (1997). *Care the Child*, 2 Volumes. New Delhi: Discovery Publishing House. ISBN 81-7141-394-3.

Bhaskara Rao, Digumarti, Editor (1998). *Earth Summit*, 2 Volumes. New Delhi : Discovery Publishing House. ISBN 81-7141-435-4.

Bhaskara Rao, Digumarti, Editor (1998). *Adolescence Education.* New Delhi : Discovery Publishing House. ISBN 81-7141-432-X.

Bhaskara Rao, Digumarti, Editor (1998). *Community and School Nutrition Education.* New Delhi : Discovery Publishing House. ISBN 81-7141-435-4.

Bhaskara Rao, Digumarti, Editor (1998). *District Primary Education Programme.* New Delhi: Discovery Publishing House. ISBN 81-7141-396-X.

Bhaskara Rao, Digumarti, Editor (1998). *National Policy on Education: Towards an Enlightened and Humane Society.* New Delhi : Discovery Publishing House. ISBN 81-7141-426-5.

Bhaskara Rao, Digumarti, Editor (1998). *Reforming School Education.* New Delhi : Discovery Publishing House. ISBN 81-7141-403-6.

Bhaskara Rao, Digumarti, Editor (1998). *Teacher Education in India.* New Delhi : Discovery Publishing House. ISBN 81-7141-406-0.

Bhaskara Rao, Digumarti, Editor (1998). *World Summit for Social Development.* New Delhi : Discovery Publishing House. ISBN 81-7141-420-6.

Bhaskara Rao, Digumarti, Editor (2001). *Nuclear Materials : Issues and Concerns*, 2 Volumes. New Delhi : Discovery Publishing House. ISBN 81-7141-611-X.

Bhaskara Rao, Digumarti, Editor (2001). *Distance Education in Different Countries.* New Delhi : APH Publishing Corporation. ISBN 81-7648-229-3.

Bhaskara Rao, Digumarti, Editor (2001). *Decentralised Management of Education : Management of Education in Panchayati Raj and Municipal Bodies.* New Delhi : Discovery Publishing House. ISBN 81-7141-617-9.

Bhaskara Rao, Digumarti, Editor (2001). *Electrochemistry for Environmental Protection.* New Delhi: Discovery Publishing House. ISBN 81-7141-619-5.

Bhaskara Rao, Digumarti, Editor (2001). *Global Educational Studies.* New Delhi : Discovery Publishing House. ISBN 81-7141-616-0.

Bhaskara Rao, Digumarti, Editor (2001). *Global Synthesis of Educational Assessment.* New Delhi : Discovery Publishing House. ISBN 81-7141-613-6.

Bhaskara Rao, Digumarti, Editor (2001). *Jomtein Decade of Education.* New Delhi : Discovery Publishing House. ISBN 81-7141-618-7.

Bhaskara Rao, Digumarti, Editor (2001). *World Conference on Education for All.* New Delhi: APH Publishing Corporation. ISBN 81-7141-274-9.

Bhaskara Rao, Digumarti, Editor (2001). *World Conference on Higher Education.* New Delhi : Discovery Publishing House. ISBN 81-7141-610-1.

Bhaskara Rao, Digumarti, Editor (2001). *World Conference on Science.* New Delhi : Discovery Publishing House. ISBN 81-7141-612-8.

Bhaskara Rao, Digumarti, Editor (2003). *Inspiring Experiences in Teacher Education.* New Delhi : Discovery Publishing House. ISBN 81-7141-656-X.

Bhaskara Rao, Digumarti, Editor (2003). *International Studies in Education*, 3 volumes. New Delhi : Discovery Publishing House. ISBN 81-7141-647-0.

Bhaskara Rao, Digumarti, Editor (2003). *Military Conversion : Impact on Science and Technology.* New Delhi : Discovery Publishing House. ISBN 81-7141-578-4.

Bhaskara Rao, Digumarti, Editor (2003). *United Nations Millennium Summit.* New Delhi : Discovery Publishing House. ISBN 81-7141-632-2.

Bhaskara Rao, Digumarti, Editor (2003). *World Assembly on Aging.* New Delhi : Discovery Publishing House. ISBN 81-7141-637-3.

Bhaskara Rao, Digumarti, Editor (2003). *World Conference on Human Rights.* New Delhi: Discovery Publishing House. ISBN 81-7141-661-6.

Bhaskara Rao, Digumarti, Editor (2003). *World Education Forum.* New Delhi: Discovery Publishing House. ISBN 81-7141-639-X.

Bhaskara Rao, Digumarti, Editor (2003). *Education, Employment and Human Resource Development*. New Delhi : Discovery Publishing House. ISBN 81-7141- 681-0.

Bhaskara Rao, Digumarti, Editor (2003). *Successful Schooling*. New Delhi : Discovery Publishing House. ISBN 81-7141-677-2.

Bhaskara Rao, Digumarti, Editor (2003). *European Education and Teachers.* New Delhi: Discovery Publishing House. ISBN 81-7141-702-7.

Bhaskara Rao, Digumarti, Editor (2003). *Teachers in a Changing World.* New Delhi : Discovery Publishing House. ISBN 81-7141-694-2.

Bhaskara Rao, Digumarti, Editor (2004). *International Guidelines on Open and Distance Teacher Education*. New Delhi: Discovery Publishing House. ISBN 81-7141-777-9.

Bhaskara Rao, Digumarti, Editor (2004). *Adult Learning in the 21st Century.* New Delhi: Discovery Publishing House. ISBN 81-7141-797-3.

Bhaskara Rao, Digumarti, Editor (2004). *Educational Practices : Research and Recommendations*. New Delhi: Discovery Publishing House. ISBN 81-7141-835-X.

Bhaskara Rao, Digumarti, Editor (2004). *General Secondary Education In the 21st Century*. New Delhi: Discovery Publishing House.

Bhaskara Rao, Digumarti, Editor (2004). *Reforming Secondary Education.* New Delhi: Discovery Publishing House. ISBN 81-7141-843-0.

Bhaskara Rao, Digumarti, Editor (2004). *Human Rights Education.* New Delhi : Discovery Publishing House. ISBN 81-7141-882-1.

Bhaskara Rao, Digumarti, Editor (2004). *United Nations Decade for Human Rights Education.* New Delhi : Discovery Publishing House. ISBN 81-7141- 887-2.

Bhaskara Rao, Digumarti, Editor (2004). *Technical and Vocational Education and Training in the 21st Century.* New Delhi : Discovery Publishing House. ISBN 81-7141- 984-4.

Bhaskara Rao, Digumarti, Editor (2005). *Encyclopaedia of Education For All,* 5 Volumes. New Delhi : Discovery Publishing House.

Bhaskara Rao, Digumarti and B.S.V. Dutt, Editors (2003). *Education : Programmes and Policies.* New Delhi : APH Publishing Corporation. ISBN 81-7648-470-9.

Bhaskara Rao, Digumarti, C.A.P. Swamy and B.S.V. Dutt (1997). *Self-Evaluation in Student Teaching.* New Delhi : Discovery Publishing House. ISBN 81-7141-374-9.

Bhaskara Rao, Digumarti and C.D. Swarna Lattha, Editors (2006). *Encyclopaedia of Biotechnology*, 5 Volumes. New Delhi : Discovery Publishing House. ISBN 81-8356-168-3 (set).

Bhaskara Rao, Digumarti, C. Sridevi and K. Vijaya (1995). *Achievement in Social Studies.* New Delhi: Discovery Publishing House. ISBN 81-7141-281-5.

Bhaskara Rao, Digumarti and D. Naresh Kumar (2004). *School Teacher Effectiveness.* New Delhi : Discovery Publishing House. ISBN 81-7141-782-5.

Bhaskara Rao, Digumarti and D. Sridhar (2002). *Job Satisfaction of School Teachers.* New Delhi : Discovery Publishing House. ISBN 81-7141-652-7.

Bhaskara Rao, Digumarti and Digumarti Pushpa Latha, Editors (1998). *International Encyclopaedia of Women*, 5 Volumes. New Delhi : Discovery Publishing House. ISBN 81-7141-410-9 (set).

Vol. 1 *Status of World's Women*. ISBN 81-7141- 494-X.

Vol. 2 *Women, Education and Empowerment.* ISBN 81-7141-498-1.

Vol. 3 *Women Challenges and Advancement.* ISBN 81-7141-497-4.

Vol. 4 *Women and Family Health.* ISBN 81-7141-497-4.

Vol. 5 *Women and International Action.* ISBN 81-7141-498-2.

Babu, P.C., Author and Digumarti Bhaskara Rao, Editor (2004). *Flowers of Wisdom.* New Delhi : Discovery Publishing House. ISBN 81-7141-695-0.

Babu, P.C., Author and Digumarti Bhaskara Rao, Editor (2008). *Worlds of Wisdom.* New Delhi: Discovery Publishing House.

Bhagya Lakshmi, L., Author and Digumarti Bhaskara Rao, Editor (2000). *Reading and Comprehension.* New Delhi : Discovery Publishing House. ISBN 81-7141-543-1.

Bhasha, S.A., Author and Digumarti Bhaskara Rao, Editor (2004). *Methods of Teaching Geography.* New Delhi : Discovery Publishing House. ISBN 81-7141-807-4.

Bhaskara Rao, Digumarti (1986). *Dhrushya Sravana Bodhanapakaranalu* (Audio Visual Teaching Aids). Guntur : Nagarjuna Publishers.

Bhaskara Rao, Digumarti (1993). *Jeevasashtra Bodhana* (Teaching of Biology). Guntur : Nagarjuna Publishers.

Bhaskara Rao, Digumarti (1994). *Vidya Manovignana Sastram* (Educational Psychology). Guntur : Nagarjuna Publishers.

Bhaskara Rao, Digumarti (1995). *Vignanasasthra Bodhana* (Teaching of science) Guntur : Nagarjuna Publishers.

Bhaskara Rao, Digumarti (1997). *Vidya Manovignana Sastram* (Educational Psychology). Guntur : Creative Press.

Bhaskara Rao, Digumarti (1998). *DSC Study Material.* Guntur : Nagarjuna Publishers.

Bhaskara Rao, Digumarti (1998). *Upadhyayudu Vidya.* (Teacher and Education) Guntur: Nagarjuna Publishers.

Bhaskara Rao, Digumarti (1998). *Vidya Drukpadalu* (Perspectives of Education). Guntur: Nagarjuna Publishers.

Bhaskara Rao, Digumarti (1999). *EdCET Teaching Aptitude.* Guntur : Nagarjuna Publishers.

Bhaskara Rao, Digumarti (2001). *Bharata Samajamulo Upadyayudu Vidhya* (Teacher and Education in Emerging Indian Society). Guntur : Sri Nagarjuna Publishers.

Bhaskara Rao, Digumarti (2001). *Bhoutika Sastra Bodhana Padhatulu* (Methods of Teaching Physical Science). Guntur : Sri Nagarjuna Publishers.

Bhaskara Rao, Digumarti (2001). *Jeeva Sastra Bodhana Padhatulu* (Methods of Teaching Biology).Guntur : Sri Nagarjuna Publishers.

Bhaskara Rao, Digumarti (2001). *Vidya Manovignana Sastram* (Educational Psychology). Guntur : Sri Nagarjuna Publishers.

Bhaskara Rao, Digumarti (2003). *Patasala Yajamanyam / Paripalana* (School Management and Administration). Guntur : Sri Nagarjuna Publishers.

Bhaskara Rao, Digumarti and A. Jagadish (2009). *Vignansastra Bodhana Padhatulu* (Methods of Teaching Science).Guntur : Sri Nagarjuna Publishers.

Bhaskara Rao, Digumarti and B. Prasad Babu (2009). *Pradhamika Vidya mariyu Vileena Vidya Dhrukpadhalu* (Perspectives in Primary Education and Inclusive Education). Guntur : Sri Nagarjuna Publishers.

Bhaskara Rao, Digumarti and B. Prasad Babu (2009). *Vidya Manovignana Sastram* (Educational Psychology). Guntur : Sri Nagarjuna Publishers.

Bhaskara Rao, Digumarti and D. Naresh Kumar (2004). *School Teacher Effectiveness.* New Delhi : Discovery Publishing House. ISBN 81-7141-782-5.

Bhaskara Rao, Digumarti and Digumarthi Harshitha (2004). *Adjustment of Adolescents.* New Delhi: APH Publishing House. ISBN 81-7648-836-8.

Bhaskara Rao, Digumarti and Digumarthi Harshitha, Editors (2001). *Education in India.* New Delhi: APH Publishing House. ISBN 81-7648-207-2.

Bhaskara Rao, Digumarti and Digumarti Pushpa Latha (1994). *Achievement in Biology.* New Delhi : Discovery Publishing House. ISBN 81-7141-264-5.

Bhaskara Rao, Digumarti and Digumarti Pushpa Latha (1994). *Achievement in Science.* New Delhi : Discovery Publishing House. ISBN 81-7141-280-70.

Bhaskara Rao, Digumarti and Digumarti Pushpa Latha (1995). *Achievement in English.* New Delhi : Discovery Publishing House. ISBN 81-7141-283-1.

Bhaskara Rao, Digumarti and Digumarti Pushpa Latha (1995). *Achievement in Mathematics.* New Delhi : Discovery Publishing House. ISBN 81-7141-278-5.

Bhaskara Rao, Digumarti and Digumarti Pushpa Latha (2004). *Education for Women.* New Delhi : Discovery Publishing House. ISBN 81-7141-873-2.

Bhaskara Rao, Digumarti and E. Sreekanth Babu (2004). *Educational Interests of School Students.* New Delhi : Discovery Publishing House. ISBN 81-7141-837-6.

Bhaskara Rao, Digumarti and G. Prasanthi (2009). *Samardya Nirmanamu* (Capacity Building). Guntur : Sri Nagarjuna Publishers.

Bhaskara Rao, Digumarti and K. Subba Rao (2009). *Elementary Vidya, Pranalika, Yajamanyam, Upadyaya Kartavyalu* (Elementary Education, Planning, Management and Teacher Functions). Guntur : Sri Nagarjuna Publishers.

Bhaskara Rao, Digumarti and K. Vijaya (1995). *A Text Book Evaluation.* Ambala Cantt : The Associated Publishers.

Bhaskara Rao, Digumarti and K.R.S. Sambasiva Rao, Editors (1996). *Current Trends in Indian Education.* New Delhi : Discovery Publishing House. ISBN 81-7141-311-0.

Bhaskara Rao, Digumarti and M.A. Fayaz (2004). *Problems of Primary School Drop-outs.* New Delhi : Discovery Publishing House. ISBN 81-7141- 834-1.

Bhaskara Rao, Digumarti and N.V.M. Mohana Rao (2002). *Problems of Mentally Handicapped Children.* New Delhi: Discovery Publishing House. ISBN 81-7141- 645-4.

Bhaskara Rao, Digumarti and S. Chandra Mohan (2002). *Sports Management.* New Delhi : APH Publishing House. ISBN 81-7648-467-9.

Bhaskara Rao, Digumarti and S.A. Khader (2004). *Problems of Private School Teachers.* New Delhi : Discovery Publishing Corporation. ISBN 81-7141-838-4.

Bhaskara Rao, Digumarti and S.A. Khader (2004). *School Education in India.* New Delhi : Discovery Publishing House. ISBN 81-7141-849-X.

Bhaskara Rao, Digumarti and Sk. Johni Basha (2004). *Teachers' Population Education Awareness.* New Delhi : Discovery Publishing House. ISBN 81-7141-832-5.

Bhaskara Rao, Digumarti, Digumarthi Harshitha and K.R.S. Sambasiva Rao, Editors (1999). *Advanced Biotechnology.* New Delhi : Discovery Publishing House. ISBN 81-7141-516-4.

Bhaskara Rao, Digumarti, Digumarti Pushpa Latha and Digumarthi Harshitha, Editors (2001). *Biological Warfare.* New Delhi: Discovery Publishing House. ISBN 81-7141-597-0.

Bhaskara Rao, Digumarti, Digumarti Pushpa Latha and Digumarthi Harshitha, Editors (2001). *Women as Educators.* New Delhi: Discovery Publishing House. ISBN 81-7141-602-0.

Bhaskara Rao, Digumarti, Digumarti Pushpa Latha and Digumarthi Harshitha, Editors (2001). *Assessing Learning Achievement.* New Delhi : Discovery Publishing House. ISBN 81-7141-601-2.

Bhaskara Rao, Digumarti, Digumarti Pushpa Latha and Digumarthi Harshitha, Editors (2001). *Energy Security.* New Delhi : Discovery Publishing House. ISBN 81-7141-598-9.

Bhaskara Rao, Digumarti, Editor (2010). *Elementary Vidya, Pranalika, Yajamanyam, Upadyaya Kartavyalu – Question Bank* (Elementary Education, Planning, Management and Teacher Functions). Guntur: Sri Nagarjuna Publishers.

Bhaskara Rao, Digumarti, Editor (2010). *Ganithasastra Bodhana Padhatulu – Question Bank* (Methods of Teaching Science).Guntur : Sri Nagarjuna Publishers.

Bhaskara Rao, Digumarti, Editor (2010). *Methods of Teaching English – Question Bank.* Guntur : Sri Nagarjuna Publishers.

Bhaskara Rao, Digumarti, Editor (2010). *Pradhamika Vidya mariyu Vileena Vidya Dhrukpadhalu – Question Bank* (Perspectives in Primary Education and Inclusive Education). Guntur : Sri Nagarjuna Publishers.

Bhaskara Rao, Digumarti, Editor (2010). *Samardya Nirmanamu – Question Bank* (Capacity Building). Guntur : Sri Nagarjuna Publishers.

Bhaskara Rao, Digumarti, Editor (2010). *Sanghikasastra Bodhana Padhatulu – Question Bank* (Methods of Teaching Social Studies).Guntur : Sri Nagarjuna Publishers.

Bhaskara Rao, Digumarti, Editor (2010). *Telugu Bodhana Padhatulu – Question Bank* (Methods of Teaching Social Studies).Guntur : Sri Nagarjuna Publishers.

Bhaskara Rao, Digumarti, Editor (2010). *Vidya Manovignana Sastram – Question Bank* (Educational Psychology). Guntur : Sri Nagarjuna Publishers.

Bhaskara Rao, Digumarti, Editor (2010). *Vignansastra Bodhana Padhatulu – Question Bank* (Methods of Teaching Science).Guntur : Sri Nagarjuna Publishers.

Bhaskara Rao, Digumarti, N. Saraja, J. Lalitha and V. Mrunalini, Translators (2008). *Vidya – Samajam (Education - Society). Hyderabad* : Dr. B.R. Ambedkar Open University.

Bhaskara Rao, Digumarti, V.V. Rao, V.V. Lakshmi and V.V. Krishna, Editors (1999). *Status and Advancement of Women.* New Delhi: APH Publishing Corporation. ISBN 81-7648-169-6.

Bhuvaneswara Lakshmi, G. and K. Subba Rao, Authors and Digumarti Bhaskara Rao, Editor (2004). *Methods of Teaching Biology.* New Delhi : Discovery Publishing House. ISBN 81-7141-914-3.

Bhuvaneswara Lakshmi, G., Author and Digumarti Bhaskara Rao, Editor (2004). *Methods of Teaching Life Science.* New Delhi : Discovery Publishing House. ISBN 81-7141-804-X.

Bhuvaneswara Lakshmi, Gadde, Author and Digumarti Bhaskara Rao, Editor (2000). *Attitude Towards Science.* New Delhi : Discovery Publishing House. ISBN 81-7141-541-6.

Bujji Babu, K., Author and Digumarti Bhaskara Rao, Editor (2007). *Teaching Aptitude of Primary School Teachers.* New Delhi: Sonali Publications. ISBN 81-8411-083-9.

Chary, K.V.N.B., Author and Digumarti Bhaskara Rao, Editor (2006). *Techniques of Teaching Physics.* New Delhi : Sonali Publications. ISBN 81-8411-046-4.

Chowdary, S.B.J.R. and Naga Raju, Authors and Digumarti Bhaskara Rao, Editor (2004). *Mastery of Teaching Skills.* New Delhi : Discovery Publishing House. ISBN 81-7141-861-9.

Dayakara Reddy, V. and Digumarti Bhaskara Rao, Editors (2006). *Value-Oriented Education.* New Delhi: Discovery Publishing House. ISBN 81-8356-051-2.

Devraj, T.A.S., Author and Digumarti Bhaskara Rao, Editor (1997). *Trace Analysis of Uranium and Thorium.* New Delhi : Discovery Publishing House. ISBN 81-7141-375-7.

Digumarti Bhaskara Rao and M. Srihari (2009). *Vardamana Bharata Desamulo Vidya* (Education in Emerging India). Guntur: Sri Nagarjuna Publishers.

Digumarti Bhaskara Rao, Editor (2010). *Vardamana Bharata Desamulo Vidya – Question Bank* (Education in Emerging India). Guntur : Sri Nagarjuna Publishers.

Durga Rani, K., Author and Digumarti Bhaskara Rao, Editor (2000). *Educational Aspirations and Scientific Attitudes.* New Delhi : Discovery Publishing House. ISBN 81-7141-555-5.

Dutt, B.S.V. and Digumarti Bhaskara Rao (2001). *Empowering Primary Teachers.* New Delhi : Discovery Publishing House. ISBN 81-7141-615-2.

Dutt, B.S.V., Author and Digumarti Bhaskara Rao, Editor (2004). *Comparative Education.* New Delhi: Discovery Publishing House. ISBN 81-7141-912-7.

Ediger, Marlow and Digumarti Bhaskara Rao (1996). *Science Curriculum.* New Delhi: Discovery Publishing House. ISBN 81-7141-321-8.

Ediger, Marlow and Digumarti Bhaskara Rao (2000). *Teaching Mathematics Successfully.* New Delhi : Discovery Publishing House. ISBN 81-7141-552-0.

Ediger, Marlow and Digumarti Bhaskara Rao (2001). *Teaching Science Successfully.* New Delhi : Discovery Publishing House. ISBN 81-7141-600-4.

Ediger, Marlow and Digumarti Bhaskara Rao (2001). *Teaching Social Studies Successfully.* New Delhi : Discovery Publishing House. ISBN 81-7141-596-2.

Ediger, Marlow and Digumarti Bhaskara Rao (2002). *Elementary Curriculum.* New Delhi : Discovery Publishing House. ISBN 81-7141-658-6.

Ediger, Marlow and Digumarti Bhaskara Rao (2002). *Improving School Administration.* New Delhi : Discovery Publishing House. ISBN 81-7141-633-0

Ediger, Marlow and Digumarti Bhaskara Rao (2002). *Philosophy and Curriculum.* New Delhi: Discovery Publishing House. ISBN 81-7141-631-4.

Ediger, Marlow and Digumarti Bhaskara Rao (2003). *Elementary Curriculum Improvement.* New Delhi : Discovery Publishing House. ISBN 81-7141-740-X.

Ediger, Marlow and Digumarti Bhaskara Rao (2003). *Language Arts Curriculum.* New Delhi : Discovery Publishing House. ISBN 81-7141-657-8.

Ediger, Marlow and Digumarti Bhaskara Rao (2003). *Psychology and Curriculum.* New Delhi : Discovery Publishing House. ISBN 81-7141-691-8.

Ediger, Marlow and Digumarti Bhaskara Rao (2003). *School Curriculum and Administration.* New Delhi : Discovery Publishing House. ISBN 81-7141-709-4.

Ediger, Marlow and Digumarti Bhaskara Rao (2003). *School Curriculum and Administration.* New Delhi : Discovery Publishing House. ISBN 81-7141-709-4.

Ediger, Marlow and Digumarti Bhaskara Rao (2003). *Teaching Language Arts Successfully.* New Delhi : Discovery Publishing House. ISBN 81-7141-678-0.

Ediger, Marlow and Digumarti Bhaskara Rao (2003). *Teaching Mathematics in Elementary Schools.* New Delhi : Discovery Publishing House. ISBN 81-7141-687-X.

Ediger, Marlow and Digumarti Bhaskara Rao (2003). *Teaching Science in Elementary Schools.* New Delhi: Discovery Publishing House. ISBN 81-7141-698-5.

Ediger, Marlow and Digumarti Bhaskara Rao (2004). *Relevancy in Elementary Curriculum.* New Delhi : Discovery Publishing House. ISBN 81-7141-845-9.

Ediger, Marlow and Digumarti Bhaskara Rao (2004). *School Organisation.* New Delhi : Discovery Publishing House. ISBN 81-7141-843-0.

Ediger, Marlow and Digumarti Bhaskara Rao (2005). *Quality School Education.* New Delhi : Discovery Publishing House. ISBN 81-8356-022-9.

Ediger, Marlow and Digumarti Bhaskara Rao (2006). *Administration of Schools.* New Delhi : Discovery Publishing House. ISBN 81-8356-244-2.

Ediger, Marlow and Digumarti Bhaskara Rao (2006). *Community College – Curriculum and Teaching.* New Delhi : Discovery Publishing House. ISBN 81-8356-053-9.

Ediger, Marlow and Digumarti Bhaskara Rao (2006). *Curriculum of School Subjects.* New Delhi: Discovery Publishing House.

Ediger, Marlow and Digumarti Bhaskara Rao (2006). *Curriculum Organisation.* New Delhi: Discovery Publishing House. ISBN 81-8356-205-1.

Ediger, Marlow and Digumarti Bhaskara Rao (2006). *Issues in School Curruculum.* New Delhi : Discovery Publishing House. ISBN 81-8356-052-0.

Ediger, Marlow and Digumarti Bhaskara Rao (2006). *Reading Curriculum and Instruction.* New Delhi : Discovery Publishing House. ISBN 81-8356-266-3.

Ediger, Marlow and Digumarti Bhaskara Rao (2006). *Successful School Education.* New Delhi : Discovery Publishing House. ISBN 81-8356-054-7.

Ediger, Marlow and Digumarti Bhaskara Rao (2006). *Successful School Administration.* New Delhi: Discovery Publishing House. ISBN 81-8356-046-6.

Ediger, Marlow and Digumarti Bhaskara Rao (2007). *Language Arts Education.* New Delhi : Discovery Publishing House. ISBN 81-8356-333-3.

Ediger, Marlow and Digumarti Bhaskara Rao (2007). *School Science Education.* New Delhi : Discovery Publishing House. ISBN 81-8356-352-X.

Ediger, Marlow and Digumarti Bhaskara Rao (2010). *Effective Schooling.* New Delhi : Discovery Publishing House. ISBN 978-81-8356-613-1.

Ediger, Marlow and Digumarti Bhaskara Rao (2010). *Effective School Curriculum.* New Delhi : Discovery Publishing House. ISBN 978-81-8356-585-1.

Ediger, Marlow and Digumarti Bhaskara Rao (2011). *Essays on Teaching Science.* New Delhi : Discovery Publishing House. ISBN 978-81-8356-882-1.

Ediger, Marlow and Digumarti Bhaskara Rao (2011). *Essays on Teaching Social Studies.* New Delhi: Discovery Publishing House Pvt. Ltd. ISBN 978-81-8356-883-8.

Ediger, Marlow and Digumarti Bhaskara Rao (2011). *Essays on Teaching Reading.* New Delhi : Discovery Publishing House Pvt. Ltd. ISBN

Ediger, Marlow and Digumarti Bhaskara Rao (2010). *Essays on Teaching Mathematics.* New Delhi : Discovery Publishing House.

Ediger, Marlow and Digumarti Bhaskara Rao (2010). *Essays on Teaching and Learning.* New Delhi : Discovery Publishing House.

Ediger, Marlow and Digumarti Bhaskara Rao, Editors (2006). *Encyclopaedia of School Education*, 5 volumes. New Delhi : Discovery Publishing House. ISBN 81-8356-308-2 (set).

Ediger, Marlow and Digumarti Bhaskara Rao, Editors (2006). *Encyclopaedia of School Administration*, 4 volumes. New Delhi : Discovery Publishing House. ISBN 81-8356-307-4 (set).

Ediger, Marlow and Digumarti Bhaskara Rao, Editors (2007). *Encyclopaedia of School Curriculum*, 10 volumes. New Delhi : Discovery Publishing House. ISBN 81-8356-305-8 (set).

Ediger, Marlow and Digumarti Bhaskara Rao, Editors (2007). *Encyclopaedia of Teaching*, 8 volumes. New Delhi : Discovery Publishing House. ISBN 81-8356-305-8 (set).

Ediger, Marlow, B.S.V. Dutt and Digumarti Bhaskara Rao (2003). *Teaching English Successfully*. New Delhi : Discovery Publishing House. ISBN 81-7141-707-8.

Elizabeth, M.E.S., Author and Digumarti Bhaskara Rao, Editor (2004). *Methods of Teaching English*. New Delhi : Discovery Publishing House. ISBN 81-7141-809-0.

Elizabeth, M.E.S., Author and Digumarti Bhaskara Rao, Editor (2004). *Acquisition of English Vocabulary*. New Delhi : Discovery Publishing House. ISBN 81-075-X .

Fatima, Sk. and Digumarti Bhaskara Rao (2008). *Reasoning Ability of Adolescent Students*. New Delhi : Sonali Publications.

Fatima, Sk. Author and Digumarti Bhaskara Rao, Editor (2007). *Reasoning Ability of School Students*. New Delhi: Discovery Publishing House. ISBN 81-8356-330-9.

G.E.P. Sastry and G. Satya Narayana, Authors, Bhaskara Rao, Digumarti, Editor (2009). *Sanghikasastra Bodhana Padhatulu* (Methods of Teaching Social Studies).Guntur : Sri Nagarjuna Publishers.

Gopala Krishna, G., A. Rama Krishna, K. Subba Rao and Bhaskara Rao, Digumarti (2004). *Jeevasashtra Bodhana Padhatulu* (Methods of Teaching of Biological Science). Guntur : Sri Nagarjuna Publishers.

Gopala Krishna, M., Author and Digumarti Bhaskara Rao, Editor (2007). *Techniques of Teaching Physical Education*. New Delhi : Sonali Publications. ISBN 81-8411-044-8.

Gopala Krishna, M., Author and Digumarti Bhaskara Rao, Editor (2007). *Techniques of Teaching Education*. New Delhi : Sonali Publications. ISBN 81-8411-062-6.

Harshitha, Digumarthi, Author and Digumarti Bhaskara Rao, Editor (2004). *Methods of Teaching Information Technology*. New Delhi: Discovery Publishing House. ISBN 81-7141-805-8.

Harshitha, Digumarthi, Author and Digumarti Bhaskara Rao, Editor (2007). *Techniques of Teaching Computer Science*. New Delhi : Sonali Publications. ISBN 81-8411-036-7.

Indira Devi, Author and J. Prasanth Kumar and Digumarti Bhaskara Rao, Editors (2004). *Values in Language Text Books.* New Delhi : Discovery Publishing House. ISBN 81-7141-833-3.

Jalaja Kumari, C., Author and Digumarti Bhaskara Rao, Editor (2004). *Methods of Teaching Educational Technology.* New Delhi : Discovery Publishing House. ISBN 81-7141-810-4.

Jalaja Kumari, C., Author and Digumarti Bhaskara Rao, Editor (2007). *Job Satisfaction of Teachers.* New Delhi : Discovery Publishing House. ISBN 81 8356 329 5.

Janardhan Reddy, B., Author and Digumarti Bhaskara Rao, Editor (2006). *Techniques of Teaching Sociology.* New Delhi : Sonali Publications. ISBN 81-8411-042-1.

Jayasree, K., Author and Digumarti Bhaskara Rao, Editor (1999). *Correlates of Socialisation.* New Delhi : Discovery Publishing House. ISBN 81-7141-517-2.

Jayasree, K., Author and Digumarti Bhaskara Rao, Editor (2004). *Methods of Teaching Science.* New Delhi : Discovery Publishing House. ISBN 81-7141-801-5.

John Babu, C., Author and T.J.R. Prasad, G.M. Madhukar and Digumarti Bhaskara Rao, Editors (2004). *Problem Solving in Mathematics.* New Delhi : APH Publishing Corporation. ISBN 81-7648-273-0.

Joseph Raju, B and G.A. Anitha, Authors and Digumarti Bhaskara Rao, Editor (2004). *Population Education.* New Delhi : Sonali Publications. ISBN 81-88836-31-3.

Krishna Murthy, V., K.S. Sudheer Reddy and Digumarti Bhaskara Rao (2004). *Vidya Manovignana Sastra Adharalu* (Foundations of Educational Psychology). Guntur : Sri Nagarjuna Publishers.

Krishna, G., Author and Digumarti Bhaskara Rao, Editor (2006). *Techniques of Teaching Physical Education.* New Delhi : Discovery Publishing House. ISBN 81-8411-044-8.

Kumar Raja, G., Author and Digumarti Bhaskara Rao, Editor (2007). *Principles of Primary School.* New Delhi : Sonali Publications. ISBN 81-8411-054-5.

Lakshmi Kumari, V., Author and Digumarti Bhaskara Rao, Editor (2006). *Techniques of Teaching Home Science.* New Delhi : Discovery Publishing House. ISBN 81-8411-048-0.

Lalini, V., V. Dayakara Reddy, M. Srihari and Digumarti Bhaskara Rao (2004). *Vidya Adharalu* (Foundations of Education). Guntur : Sri Nagarjuna Publishers.

Lalitha, T., Author and K.S. Prabhakaram, D.S.N. Sastry and Digumarti Bhaskara Rao, Editors (2004). *Educational Philosophic Beliefs.* New Delhi: Discovery Publishing House. ISBN 81-7141-765-5.

Madhava, K., Author and Digumarti Bhaskara Rao, Editor (2008). *Personality of Adolescent Students.* New Delhi: Sonali Publications.

Madhu Bala, Jampala, Author and Digumarti Bhaskara Rao, Editor (2004). *Methods of Teaching Exceptional Children.* New Delhi: Discovery Publishing House. ISBN 81-7141-802-3.

Madhu Bala, Jampala, Author and Digumarti Bhaskara Rao, Editor (2007). *Adjustment, Achievement Motivation and Academic Achievement of Hearing Impaired Students.* New Delhi: Discovery Publishing House

Marja, Talvi and Digumarti Bhaskara Rao, Editors (1996). *Educational Leadership and Social Changes.* New Delhi : Discovery Publishing House. ISBN 81-7141-320-X.

Marlow Ediger and Digumarti Bhaskara Rao, Editors (2006). *Encyclopaedia of School Education*, 5 volumes. New Delhi : Discovery Publishing House. ISBN 81-8356-308-2 (set).

Marlow Ediger and Digumarti Bhaskara Rao, Editors (2006). *Encyclopaedia of School Administration*, 4 volumes. New Delhi : Discovery Publishing House. ISBN 81-8356-307-4 (set).

Marlow Ediger and Digumarti Bhaskara Rao, Editors (2007). *Encyclopaedia of School Curriculum*, 10 volumes. New Delhi : Discovery Publishing House. ISBN 81-8356-305-8 (set).

Marlow Ediger and Digumarti Bhaskara Rao, Editors (2007). *Encyclopaedia of Teaching*, 8 volumes. New Delhi : Discovery Publishing House. ISBN 81-8356-305-8 (set).

Naga Kumari, U., Author and Digumarti Bhaskara Rao, Editor (2008). *Science Process Skills of School Students.* New Delhi : Sonali Publications.

Nageswara Rao, S. and M. Srihari, Authors and Digumarti Bhaskara Rao, Editor (2004). *Guidance and Counselling.* New Delhi : Discovery Publishing House. ISBN 81-7141-840-6.

Nageswara Rao, S. and P. Sridhar, Authors and Digumarti Bhaskara Rao, Editor (2004). *Methods and Techniques of Teaching.* New Delhi : Sonali Publications. ISBN 81-88836-33-8.

Nageswara Rao, S., Author and Digumarti Bhaskara Rao, Editor (2006). *Techniques of Teaching Psychology.* New Delhi : Discovery Publishing House. ISBN 81-8411-040-5.

Nirmala Jyothi, M., Author and Digumarti Bhaskara Rao, Editor (2003). *Non-detention System in School Education.* New Delhi : Discovery Publishing House. ISBN 81-7141-654-3.

Padma Tulasi, G., Author and Digumarti Bhaskara Rao, Editor (2004). *Methods of Teaching Elementary Science.* New Delhi : Discovery Publishing House. ISBN 81-7141-871-6.

Pala Prasada Rao, V., Author and D. Bhaskara Rao, Editors (2008). *Functioning of Autonomous Colleges.* New Delhi : Sonali Publications.

Pala Prasada Rao, V., Author and K. N. Rani and D. Bhaskara Rao, Editors (2004). *India Pakistan : Partition Perspectives in Indo English Novels.* New Delhi: Discovery Publishing House. ISBN 81-7141-871-6.

Pitchi Reddy, M., Author and Digumarti Bhaskara Rao, Editor (2007). *Techniques of Teaching Social Sciences.* New Delhi : Sonali Publications. ISBN 81-8411-066-X.

Prabhakaram, K.S., Author and Digumarti Bhaskara Rao, Editors (1998). *Concept Attainment Model in Mathematics Teaching.* New Delhi : Discovery Publishing House. ISBN 81-7141-424-9.

Prasad Babu, B., Author and M.V.R. Raju and Digumarti Bhaskara Rao, Editors (2006). *Behavioural Problems of School Children.* New Delhi: Discovery Publishing House. ISBN 81-8356-206-X.

Prasad Babu, B., Author and P. Madhu and Digumarti Bhaskara Rao, Editors (2006). *Psychological Adjustment and Well-being.* New Delhi: Discovery Publishing House. ISBN 81-8356-204-3.

Prasanth Kumar, J., Author and Digumarti Bhaskara Rao, Editor (1998). *Effectiveness of Distance Education System.* New Delhi : Discovery Publishing House. ISBN 81-7141-437-0.

Prasanth Kumar, J., Author and Digumarti Bhaskara Rao, Editor (2004). *Methods of Teaching Civics.* New Delhi : Discovery Publishing House. ISBN 81-7141-806-6.

Prasanth Kumar, J., Author and G. Sundara Rao and Digumarti Bhaskara Rao, Editors (2000). *Open University Student Support Services.* New Delhi : Discovery Publishing House. ISBN 81-7141-550-4.

Raja Kumari, M.A. and D.R.S. Sundari, Authors and Digumarti Bhaskara Rao, Editor (2004). *Special Education.* New Delhi : Discovery Publishing House. ISBN 81-7141-846-5.

Raja Kumari, M.A. and D.R.S. Sundari, Authors and Digumarti Bhaskara Rao, Editor (2004). *Methods of Teaching Educational Psychology.* New Delhi : Discovery Publishing House. ISBN 81-7141-820-1.

Rama Krishna Prasad and P. Vide Sagar, Authors and Digumarti Bhaskara Rao, Editor (2004). *Methods of Teaching Physical Education.* New Delhi: Discovery Publishing House.

Rama Krishnaiah, D., Author and Digumarti Bhaskara Rao, Editor (1998). *Job Satisfaction of College Teachers.* New Delhi : Discovery Publishing House. ISBN 81-7141-438-9.

Rama Kumar Ratnam, M.V., Author and Digumarti Bhaskara Rao, Editor (1998). *Dukkha : Suffering in Early Buddhism.* New Delhi: Discovery Publishing House. ISBN 81-7141-653-5.

Rama Seshaiah, P. Author and Digumarti Bhaskara Rao, Editor (2004). *Methods of Teaching Home Science.* New Delhi : Discovery Publishing House. ISBN 81-7141-916-X.

Rama Swamy, K., Author and Digumarti Bhaskara Rao, Editor (2007). *Techniques of Teaching Environmental Science.* New Delhi : Sonali Publications. ISBN 81-8411-035-9.

Ramatulasamma, K., Author and Digumarti Bhaskara Rao, Editor (2002). *Job Satisfaction of Teacher Educators.* New Delhi : Discovery Publishing House. ISBN 81-7141-655-1.

Ramesh, A.R., Author and Digumarti Bhaskara Rao, Editor (2006). *Techniques of Teaching Commerce.* New Delhi: Sonali Publications. ISBN 81-8411-043-X.

Ramesh, Ghanta and Digumarti Bhaskara Rao, Editors (1998). *Environmental Education: Problems and Prospects.* New Delhi: Discovery Publishing House. ISBN 81-7141-423-0.

Ranga Rao, B., Author and Digumarti Bhaskara Rao, Editor (2007). *Techniques of Teaching Economics.* New Delhi : Sonali Publications. ISBN 81-8411-056-1..

Ranga Rao, R., Author and Digumarti Bhaskara Rao, Editor (2004). *Methods of Teacher Teaching.* New Delhi : Discovery Publishing House. ISBN 81-7141-812-0.

Rani, S.S., Author and Digumarti Bhaskara Rao, Editor (2006). *Techniques of Teaching Botany.* New Delhi : Discovery Publishing House. ISBN 81-8411-037-5.

Rathaiah, Lavu and Digumarti Bhaskara Rao (1997). *Achievement Correlates.* New Delhi: Discovery Publishing House. ISBN 81-7141-385-4.

Rathaiah, Lavu and Digumarti Bhaskara Rao, Editors (1996), *International Innovations in Education.* New Delhi : Discovery Publishing House. ISBN 81-7141-359-5.

Ravi Krishna, M., Author and Digumarti Bhaskara Rao, Editor (2004). *Examination System.* New Delhi : Discovery Publishing House. ISBN 81-7141-824-4.

Ravi Kumar, M., Author and Digumarti Bhaskara Rao, Editor (2004). *Methods of Teaching Computer Science.* New Delhi : Discovery Publishing House. ISBN 81-7141-823-6.

Rudramamba, B. and V. Lakshmi Kumari, Authors and Digumarti Bhaskara Rao, Editor (2004). *Methods of Teaching Economics.* New Delhi : Discovery Publishing House. ISBN 81-7141-900-3.

Rudramamba, B., Author and Digumarti Bhaskara Rao, Editor (2003). *Problems of Teaching.* New Delhi : APH Publishing Corporation. ISBN 81-7648-462-8.

Sambasiva Rao, P., Author and Digumarti Bhaskara Rao, Editor (2007). *Techniques of Teaching Psychology.* New Delhi : Sonali Publications. ISBN 81-8411-040-5.

Sanjeeva Rao, P.C., Author and Digumarti Bhaskara Rao, Editor (1996). *A Text Book of Geology.* New Delhi : Discovery Publishing House. ISBN 81-7141-313-7.

Santhanam, T., B. Prasad Babu and S. Sugandhi, Authors and Digumarti Bhaskara Rao, Editor (2007). *Children with Learning Disabilities.* New Delhi : Sonali Publications. ISBN 81-8411-077-4.

Santhanam, T., B. Prasad Babu and S. Sugandhi, Authors and Digumarti Bhaskara Rao, Editor (2008). *Learning Disabilities and Remedial Programmes.* New Delhi : Discovery Publishing House.

Sarala, M.M.O., Author and Digumarti Bhaskara Rao, Editor (2006). *Techniques of Teaching English.* New Delhi : Sonali Publications. ISBN 81-8411-047-2.

Satya Narayana, G., Author and Digumarti Bhaskara Rao, Editor (2008). *Attitude Towards Social Studies and Achievement in Social Studies.* New Delhi : Sonali Publications.

Satya Narayana, P.V.V. and G. Krishna, Authors and Digumarti Bhaskara Rao, Editor (2004). *Curriculum Development and Management.* New Delhi : Discovery Publishing House. ISBN 81-7141-813-9.

Satya Narayana, V., Author and Digumarti Bhaskara Rao, Editor (2001). *Physical Education, Social Attitudes and Leadership Qualities.* New Delhi: Discovery Publishing House. ISBN 81-7141-593-8.

Shamsuddin, Sk. and V. Dayakara Reddy, Authors and Digumarti Bhaskara Rao, Editor (2007). *Academic Achievement and Values.* New Delhi : Discovery Publishing House.

Singh, Y.C., Author and Digumarti Bhaskara Rao, Editor (2006). *Techniques of Teaching Science.* New Delhi : Sonali Publications. ISBN 81-8411-041-3.

Sirisha Rani, S., Author and Digumarti Bhaskara Rao, Editor (2007). *Techniques of Teaching Botany.* New Delhi : Sonali Publications. ISBN 81-8411-037-5.

Siva Lakshmi, G.V. and G.L. Subbaiah, Authors and Digumarti Bhaskara Rao, Editor (2004). *Methods of Teaching Environmental Science.* New Delhi: Discovery Publishing House. ISBN 81-7141-839-2.

Sivaratnam Reddy, M., Author and Digumarti Bhaskara Rao, Editor (2004). *Creativity in College Students.* New Delhi : Discovery Publishing House. ISBN 81-7141-697-7.

Srihari, M., Author and Digumarti Bhaskara Rao, Editor (2003). *Values of Prospective Teachers.* New Delhi : Discovery Publishing House. ISBN 81-8356-328-7.

Srinivas Rao, P., Author and Digumarti Bhaskara Rao, Editor (2007). *Principles of Secondary School.* New Delhi : Sonali Publications. ISBN 81-8411-058-8.

Srinivas, G. and Digumarti Bhaskara Rao (2007). *Anxiety of Prospective Teachers.* New Delhi : Sonali Publications. ISBN 81-8411-084-7.

Srinivas, M. and I. Prasada Rao, Authors and Digumarti Bhaskara Rao, Editor (2004). *Methods of Teaching History.* New Delhi : Discovery Publishing House. ISBN 81-7141-803 1.

Srinivasa Rao, Mandalapu, Author and Digumarti Bhaskara Rao, Editor (2003). *Achievement Motivation and Achievement in Mathematics.* New Delhi : Discovery Publishing House. ISBN 81-7141-674-8.

Srinivasulu Reddy, M. and K.R.S. Sambasiva Rao, Authors and Digumarti Bhaskara Rao, Editor (1999). *A Text Book of Aquaculture.* New Delhi : Discovery Publishing House. ISBN 81-7141-482-6.

Subba Rao, K., Author and Digumarti Bhaskara Rao, Editor (2007). *School Education Policy.* New Delhi : Discovery Publishing House. ISBN 81-8356-285-X.

Subba Rao, K., Author and Digumarti Bhaskara Rao, Editor (2007). *Education Planning.* New Delhi : Sonali Publications. ISBN 81-8411-053-7.

Subba Rao, K.P., P. Ayodhya and Digumarti Bhaskara Rao (2004). *Patasala Yajamanyam – Vidhya Vyavasthalu* (School Management and Systems of Education). Guntur : Sri Nagarjuna Publishers.

Sudhakar Reddy, Y., Author and Digumarti Bhaskara Rao, Editor (2003). *Creativity in Adolescents.* New Delhi : Discovery Publishing House. ISBN 81-7141-659-4.

Sudhakar, V., B. Ravindra Babu, D.S. Kumar and Digumarti Bhaskara Rao (2004). *Vidya Sanketika Sastram - Computer Vidhya* (Educational Technology and Computer Education). Guntur : Sri Nagarjuna Publishers.

Suneetha, G., Author and Digumarti Bhaskara Rao, Editor (2004). *Environmental Awareness of School Students.* New Delhi : Sonali Publications. ISBN 81-8411-085-5.

Sunil Kumar, K. and K. Rama Krishana, Authors and Digumarti Bhaskara Rao, Editor (2004). *Methods of Teaching Chemistry.* New Delhi : Discovery Publishing House. ISBN 81-7141-913-5.

Sunita, E. and R. Sambasiva Rao, Authors and Digumarti Bhaskara Rao, Editor (2004). *Methods of Teaching Mathematics.* New Delhi : Discovery Publishing House. ISBN 81-7141-915-1.

Surya Madhava, I., Author and Digumarti Bhaskara Rao, Editor (2006). *Techniques of Teaching Geography.* New Delhi : Discovery Publishing House. ISBN 81-8411-034-0.

Surya Madhava, I., Author and Digumarti Bhaskara Rao, Editor (2007). *Techniques of Teaching Political Science.* New Delhi : Discovery Publishing House. ISBN 81-8411-061-8.

Swamy, K.R., Author and Digumarti Bhaskara Rao, Editor (2006). *Techniques of Teaching Environmental Science.* New Delhi : Discovery Publishing House. ISBN 81-8411-035-9.

Swarna Jyothi, K., Author and Digumarti Bhaskara Rao, Editor (2007). *Educational Research.* New Delhi : Sonali Publications. ISBN 81-8411-063-4.

Swarna Latha, C.D., and Digumarti Bhaskara Rao, Editors (2006). *Encyclopaedia of Biotechnology*, 5 Volumes. New Delhi : Discovery Publishing House. ISBN 81-8356-168-3.

Swarupa Rani, T. and J.R. Priyadarshini, Authors and Digumarti Bhaskara Rao, Editor (2004). *Educational Measurement and Evaluation.* New Delhi: Discovery Publishing House. ISBN 81-7141-859-7.

Valeri V. Koustiouk, Author and Digumarti Bhaskara Rao, Editor (2002). *A Text Book of Cryogenics.* New Delhi : Discovery Publishing House. ISBN 81-7141-642-X.

Vamsi Krishna, V., Author and Digumarti Bhaskara Rao, Editor (2004). *School Psychology.* New Delhi: Discovery Publishing House. ISBN 81-7141-880-5.

Vanaja, M. and N. Sneha Latha, Authors and Digumarti Bhaskara Rao, Editor (2004). *Student Shyness.* New Delhi : APH Publishing Corporation.

Vanaja, M., Author and Digumarti Bhaskara Rao, Editor (1999). *Inquiry Training Model.* New Delhi : Discovery Publishing House. ISBN 81-7141-515-6.

Vanaja, M., Author and Digumarti Bhaskara Rao, Editor (2004). *Methods of Teaching Physics.* New Delhi : Discovery Publishing House. ISBN 81-7141-867-8

Veena Kumari, Balusu and Digumarti Bhaskara Rao (1996). *Operation Black Board.* New Delhi : APH Publishing Corporation. ISBN 81-7024-711-X.

Veena Kumari, Balusu, Author and Digumarti Bhaskara Rao, Editor (2004). *Methods of Teaching Social Studies.* New Delhi : Discovery Publishing House. ISBN 81-7141-899-6.

Veena Kumari, Balusu, Author and Digumarti Bhaskara Rao, Editor (2000). *Psycho-Social Correlates of Achievement.* New Delhi : Discovery Publishing House. ISBN 81-7141-547-4.

Venkata Rao, B., Author and Digumarti Bhaskara Rao, Editor (2007). *Techniques of Teaching Chemistry.* New Delhi : Sonali Publications. ISBN 81-8411-057-X.

Venkata Rao, P. and Digumarti Bhaskara Rao (1989). *A Text Book of Zoology – Junior Intermediate.* Guntur : Vignan Publishers.

Venkata Rao, P. and Digumarti Bhaskara Rao (1989). *A Text Book of Zoology – Senior Intermediate.* Guntur : Vignan Publishers.

Venkateswara Rao, V., Author and Digumarti Bhaskara Rao, Editor (2004). *Problems of Education.* New Delhi : Discovery Publishing House. ISBN 81-7141-841-4.

Venkateswara Rao, V., V. Vijaya Lakshmi and V. Vamsi Krishna, Authors and Digumarti Bhaskara Rao, Editor (2004). *Education For All.* New Delhi : Sonali Publications. ISBN 81-88836-30-3.

Venkateswara Rao, V., V. Vijaya Lakshmi and V. Vamsi Krishna, Authors and Digumarti Bhaskara Rao, Editor (2004). *Education in India.* New Delhi : Sonali Publications. ISBN 81-88836-858-9.

Venkateswara Reddy, L. and Narayana, M. L, Authors and Digumarti Bhaskara Rao, Editor (2004). *Methods of Teaching Rural Sociology.* New Delhi : Discovery Publishing House. ISBN 81-7141-811-2.

Venkateswara Reddy, L. and Narayana, M. L., Authors and Digumarti Bhaskara Rao, Editor (2004). *Education for Dalits.* New Delhi : Discovery Publishing House. ISBN 81-7141-872-4.

Venkateswarlu, K. and S.J. Basha, Authors and Digumarti Bhaskara Rao, Editor (2004). *Methods of Teaching Commerce.* New Delhi : Discovery Publishing House. ISBN 81-7141-808-2.

Venugopala Rao, K., Author and Digumarti Bhaskara Rao, Editor (2000). *Teacher Morale in Secondary Schools.* New Delhi : Discovery Publishing House. ISBN 81-7141-551-2.

Venugopala Rao, K., Author and Digumarti Bhaskara Rao, Editor (2007). *Techniques of Teaching History.* New Delhi : Sonali Publications. ISBN 81-8411-059-6.

Vidya, C., Author and Digumarti Bhaskara Rao, Editor (1996). *A Text Book of Nutrition.* New Delhi : Discovery Publishing House. ISBN 81-7141-309-9.

Vijaya Bharathi, D., Author and Digumarti Bhaskara Rao, Editor (2000). *Educational Philosophies of Swami Vivekananda and John Dewey.* New Delhi : APH Publishing House. ISBN 81-7648-309-9.

Vijaya Bharathi, D., Author and Digumarti Bhaskara Rao, Editor (2005). *Educational Philosophy of John Dewey.* New Delhi : Discovery Publishing House. ISBN 81-8356-024-5.

Vijaya Bharathi, D., Author and Digumarti Bhaskara Rao, Editor (2005). *Educational Philosophy of Swami Vivekananda.* New Delhi : Discovery Publishing House. ISBN 81-8356-023-7.

Vijaya Kumar, S.J., Author and Digumarti Bhaskara Rao, Editor (2006). *Techniques of Teaching Mathematics.* New Delhi : Sonali Publications. ISBN 81-8411-039-1.

Vijaya Lakshmi, D., Author and Digumarti Bhaskara Rao, Editor (2004) *Basic Education.* New Delhi : Discovery Publishing House. ISBN 81-7141-881-3.

Vijaya Lakshmi, V., Author and Digumarti Bhaskara Rao, Editor (2006). *Techniques of Teaching Music.* New Delhi : Discovery Publishing House. ISBN 81-8411-038-3.

Vimala, T.D., B. Prasad Babu and Digumarti Bhaskara Rao, Editors (2007). *Stress, Coping and Management.* New Delhi : Sonali Publications. ISBN 81-8411-086-3.

Visalakshi, V., Author and Digumarti Bhaskara Rao, Editor (2006). *Techniques of Teaching Biology.* New Delhi : Sonali Publications. ISBN 81-8411-045-6.

Visalakshi, V., Author and Digumarti Bhaskara Rao, Editor (2007). *Techniques of Teaching Zoology.* New Delhi : Sonali Publications. ISBN 81-8411-055-3.

Index